PENGUIN BOOKS

ABSOLUTE ZHIRINOVSKY

Vladimir Wolfovich Zhirinovsky was born in the capital of Kazakhstan, Alma-Ata (now Almaty), in 1946. In 1964 he became a student at the Institute of Oriental Languages, in Moscow, graduating in Turkish. He later went to Turkey as part of a Soviet trade delegation but was arrested and deported by the Turkish authorities on the charge of spreading Communist propaganda, despite the fact that he was never a member of the Soviet Communist Party. After completing his compulsory military service he studied law at evening classes, getting a second degree that enabled him to secure various jobs, none of which he found particularly satisfactory.

By his own account his interest in politics dates back to his teens and earlier. He founded the Liberal Democratic Party of the Soviet Union in March 1990 and came to public prominence in 1991, when at the first-ever Soviet presidential elections he received more than 6 million votes, coming third after Boris Yeltsin and Nicolai Ryzhkev, the former Prime Minister. In December 1993 his new party, the Liberal Democratic Party of Russia, received more votes than any other single party. His declared aim is to become President of Russia as soon as possible.

Graham Frazer and George Lancelle are both experts in Russian affairs.

GRAHAM FRAZER AND **GEORGE LANCELLE**

ABSOLUTE ZHIRINOVSKY

A Transparent View of the Distinguished Russian Statesman

PENGUIN BOOKS

PENGUIN BOOKS
Published by the Penguin Group
Penguin Books USA Inc., 375 Hudson Street,
New York, New York 10014, U.S.A.
Penguin Books Ltd, 27 Wrights Lane,
London W8 5TZ, England
Penguin Books Australia Ltd, Ringwood,
Victoria, Australia
Penguin Books Canada Ltd, 10 Alcorn Avenue,
Toronto, Ontario, Canada M4V 3B2
Penguin Books (N.Z.) Ltd, 182–190 Wairau Road,
Auckland 10, New Zealand

Penguin Books Ltd, Registered Offices:
Harmondsworth, Middlesex, England

First published in Penguin Books 1994

1 3 5 7 9 10 8 6 4 2

Copyright © Graham Frazer and George Lancelle, 1994
All rights reserved

ISBN 0 14 02.4339 9
(CIP data available)

Printed in the United States of America
Set in Electra

CONTENTS

This book is intended to be a counterblast to Mao Tse-Tung's *Little Red Book*, which contains sayings of the red tyrant of China. There are differences between the two, the most obvious being that Mao's book was compiled by himself and Zhirinovsky's by us. The color black of fascism or of national socialism, as Zhirinovsky calls it, replaces the red of Communism. Also Chairman Mao was in power when he wrote it, whereas Zhirinovsky has made his statements while aspiring to supreme power.

Mao Tse-Tung and Zhirinovsky have, however, one thing in common: Neither of them seems to have been deterred by the destructive force of nuclear weapons or, more precisely, both have wanted to give the impression of not being afraid of them. Zhirinovsky has repeatedly threatened Japan and Germany, for instance, with nuclear attacks, which the rest of the world fondly hopes is mere posturing and exhibitionism, that is, a kind of hoax. Mao Tse-Tung, latter-day Chinese sage as he was, said in 1955: "The atomic hoax of the United States cannot scare the Chinese people. We have a population of 600 million, and a territory of 9.6 million square kilometers. That little bit of atomic weaponry that the United States has cannot annihilate the Chinese people. Even if the United States had more powerful atom bombs and used them on China, blasted a hole in the Earth or blew it to pieces, [while] this might be a matter of great significance to the solar system, it would still be an insignificant matter as far as the universe as a whole is concerned."[1] Mao did have original ideas.

Zhirinovsky also has original ideas; not least is he prepared to threaten nuclear first strikes but there is also, of course, his obsession of wishing Russian soldiers to wash their boots in the Indian Ocean. But these are firmly embedded in a confused jumble of present-day Russian "views": banalities. The wild ideas have to be associated with the homely, the bellicose with the blander side. As a consummate demagogue or politician, if you like (according to him, the two concepts are more or less coextensive), he has an unusually keen sense of what the prevalent prejudices, dreams, fears and aspirations are in Russia, and he tailors his pronouncements to what the audiences he addresses want to hear. As W. Lepukhin, a member of the Russian Duma, said: "Vladimir Wolfovich has no ideology. His consciousness is the same as the rest of the confused Russian reality, so it is received by the masses as revelation." (Die Zeit, 14.1.94.)

Russian banalities are to a large extent unknown in the West, and one man's banality is another man's novelty. One thing is certain: his ideas startled the West. At the moment Zhirinovsky is interested only in Russian opinions and attitudes: he has, or wants to give the impression of having, a well-developed contempt for Western and other countries, for their preferences and current views of the commonplace.

What he says abroad, apart from Serbia perhaps, serves only two purposes: to get publicity for himself in the Western media and to demonstrate to his audience back home his scorn for Western countries in particular, which are supposed to be much admired at the moment by many reformist Russian leaders, and less and less by the

[1] Xuanji, V. (Mao's Selected Works), pp. 136–7, "A Conversation between Mao and Finland's first Ambassador to China."

population, thereby also defying the respect that the West expects from a country whose social, economic and political systems have proved nonviable. His views also fly in the face of the current "informed" opinion of the reformers in Russia, who are trying to find a way out of the quagmire in which the Soviet Union landed Russia.

But perhaps most of all he brings to the surface desires in his audience that they did not know they had, which, however, correspond to their deep longings: he is a virtuoso of a demagogue.

Russia's only claim to superpower status is its military might and, in particular, its nuclear arsenal. In the words of Andrei Kozyrev, Russian Foreign Minister: "Russia is still a superpower, a nuclear superpower, a military superpower, which can probably destroy the world in thirty minutes."[2] This is perhaps a crass simplification of what the reformers in the Russian leadership think of their country's present importance in the world, a reductionism and vulgarization worthy of Zhirinovsky.

But what is the status of the set of the banalities of which Zhirinovsky is the mirror? And how does he relate his original ideas to banalities? Does he really express that body of opinion for the sole purpose of making himself popular because a large section, perhaps the majority, of the Russian population share it and like to hear it said out loud in public? How far does he take these views seriously and believe in them?

What Zhirinovsky voices in his speeches, statements and writings (when he does not happen to outline an original idea) are not so much opinions as "mental tics," such as people would conjure up when daydreaming about their country, its identity, its standing and importance in the world, and about their own identity as defined by belonging to that country, as well as the troubles which may derive from all that. These underpin the utterances a man might make in a bar after a good many glasses of vodka when rational thought is not paramount.

[2] *Call Me Hitler*, BBC 1 *Panorama*, 28.3.94.

Such "views" are determined largely by a continuing tradition that is made up of myths and realities about past history as handed down by generations up to the present time. They are complemented by individual experiences, but what really counts is the body of such shared traditions and experience, reduced to the lowest common denominator, that is, the "matters of common knowledge" that thinking people may be ashamed to voice or think unnecessary to mention, and, for that very reason, these are precisely the things that foreigners are unlikely to know. The elements in such a body of "knowledge" may vary from person to person but are sufficiently uniform to constitute a rudimentary national identity. Politicians, who share it, also take it for granted and inevitably formulate their programs taking it into consideration. Their success or failure depends to a large extent on how well they manage to incorporate it and build upon it.

There is such a body of "opinions" in every country; parts of it may be gradually covered up, shaped or eliminated as new shared knowledge and experience are absorbed by the population. When politicians are at a loss for a real opinion they may fall back upon this shared body of commonplaces, as we can see, for example, in Britain when questions of the European Union are discussed, or in Germany (problems of the *Gastarbeiter*), or in France (immigration).

We have compiled Zhirinovsky's imaginary book from his statements, speeches and writings, selecting representative views that belong to this body of "matters of common knowledge," shared prejudices and aspirations on which any populist demagogue builds his career. If Zhirinovsky falters, somebody else is likely to step into his shoes and do much the same, perhaps less outspokenly, less frankly and with much less skill, but the body of opinion reflecting that lowest common denominator in Russia will remain the same for a good while.

For in Russia all political and social thought of the past two or three generations has remained frozen by the Utopian ideology of Communism, which has been resolutely maintained by the leadership, although such faith in it as there ever was has dwindled at an ever-quickening pace. Promises and hopes have gradually proved to be hollow and vain; most of the leadership and the population have become more and more disillusioned and cynical as the gulf between theory and practice has widened. Faith and hope had, in fact, been in fairly short supply since the Stalinist period. From 1990 onward Russians have been reaching back to their pre-Communist past, dusting down many old attitudes and ideas, which, in some form or other, continued their subterranean existence under the permafrost of totalitarian Communism. As we shall see, Zhirinovsky is particularly careful to exclude the Communist tradition from his rhetoric, although neither could he help to preserve, nor did he want to discard, anything that his potential constituency has kept alive. He also has a "subtext" that may add up to giving some coherence to his practical suggestions, such as they are; there may, after all, be a "figure in the carpet"—a matter that we shall examine further in the Postscript. In the Introduction we discuss all such traditions as live on in the mind of the "common man," Zhirinovsky's "little man," with whom he resolutely identifies. The main body of this book contains his sayings, which are sometimes relevant in more than one context, with commentary where necessary.

The prevalent mood of present-day Russian society is characterized by disillusionment, resentment and despair; these are feelings on which populist demagogues like Zhirinovsky construct their platforms. To what extent can such a mood be traced back to past experience as it lives on, perhaps in a distorted or exaggerated form in the mind, and what part of it is a reaction to the present situation?

IN THE CLUTCHES OF THE PAST

"The Russians idolize the past, hate the present and fear the future," said Chekhov. Most nations do their best to make the most of their past, usually emphasizing its moments of glory or supposed happiness (the blurred outlines of distant events are the stuff that national myths are made of). Russians, however, differ from most other nations in one important respect: they seem to draw almost as much upon past misfortunes and suffering as upon past glory and happiness when they think about the present and the future. (A similar attitude can be found in Serbia: the battle of Kossovo in 1389, where the Serbs suffered a crushing defeat at the hands of the Ottoman Turkish army, resulting in four and a half centuries of Ottoman rule, is perhaps the most fêted event in Serbian history.)

Foreign invasions have for centuries weighed heavily on the Russian mind: the memory of the Tatar invasions of 1240, in particular, whose consequence, the rule of the Golden Horde, retarded the formation of a properly unified Russian state and the free development of society and culture by at least two hundred years and distorted it, perhaps for that reason, in the long run.

The Tatar invasion, has, however, left another legacy: the feeling that Europe is indebted to Russia for having saved Christian Europe from the barbarian hordes, a debt, which—it is felt in Russia—has never been repaid or even acknowledged by appropriate gratitude. The Europeans have always assumed that what saved them was the sudden death of the Great Khan in Mongolia, which prompted the invading Batu Khan to abandon the European campaign and return to Asia, and that the Teutonic Knights also played a hand at Liegnitz.

Then there were the invasions from the west: the Lithuanians, the Poles, the Germans, the Swedes, Napoleon and, finally, the Germans again in the two world wars. Russians played an important role in defeating Napoleon alongside many European nations. They were on the side of the Entente powers in the First World War, and the Soviet Union as an ally was crucially important in saving Europe from Nazi Germany in the Second World War. Although this debt has always been duly acknowledged, the Russian sense of having been short-changed has persisted. Zhirinovsky also claims that Russia saved Europe from the Ottoman Turks, but, in fact, they chose the route across the Balkans to Hungary and Vienna. The only significant invasions from the east were the Japanese ones; most invasions in north Asia were undertaken by the Russians in conquering the whole of Siberia, and later Central Asia and, nearer home, the Caucasus.

Striving for security, Russia has acquired a vast empire, for no country can ever feel absolutely safe: expansionism has become a habit, almost a complex, to which Zhirinovsky panders in his political program. But there is more to it than that.

A LAND IN SEARCH OF WARM SEAS

Zhirinovsky's expansionist program perplexes foreigners far afield and frightens neighbors. The last thing Russia needs now is more land, a Swiss or a Japanese would think: making the most of what you have is the hallmark of successful nations in history.

Russians look at the USA and Canada, on a resource-rich continent not dissimilar from their own territory, and ask themselves why they cannot be as rich. In a BBC TV *Panorama* program (28.3.94) about Zhirinovsky the journalist asked a north Russian peasant couple why they supported Zhirinovsky. The woman said the following: "Ideally, everything ought to be Russian, everything ours, home-produced. What a country this is, so much land . . . we ought to be the richest country in the world, but we're beggars, downright beggars." Zhirinovsky thinks he has got the answer for her. Sea borders are the best borders, he contends, talking of England and of its empire: "England was a sea power with the best sea borders! Mongolia has no sea borders: it is a shabby state. Today we have no colonies. The colonies provided England with the lion's share of its profit. Today we receive nothing from colonies and yet feed beggarly appendages. We should be thinking about colonies." (Clearly, Switzerland is not uppermost in Zhirinovsky's mind, whereas reflecting on Swiss history might do him and modern Russians a lot of good, since it is the very opposite of a shabby state.)

If only Russia had access to a warm ocean—which for her would have to be the Indian Ocean, or the Mediterranean at least, instead of the frozen Arctic coastline and cold Baltic shore—then at last it could be a success, becoming almost a giant peninsula with other lesser peninsulas, China, India and Indochina. Hence the logic of the Last Dash to the South.

Zhirinovsky's solution is typical of Russian history. Russia possesses reasonably warm seas already: the Caspian and the Black Sea, which gives it access to the Mediterranean and beyond it to the world's oceans. This partly explains the long tsarist quest for Constantinople. It is typical of Russians to pose their problems in terms that require solutions in the shape of extending their borders. Dissatisfied with what they have and unable to digest it properly (unlike the Swiss and the Japanese, for example), they are like peasants covetous of their neighbors' land. Not displaced persons, they are misplaced persons in their own eyes, because they live in the north and hanker after warm holiday resorts.

Zhirinovsky has a plan for combining "business" with pleasure, "business" being the occupation of new territories. He suggests that Russian troops should be issued new and better automatic weapons, which would make it possible "for any platoon of Russian soldiers to pacify any region. And what is more, that should not be an unpleasant affair. It is always necessary to bring order to these regions. So, on the shores of the Indian Ocean and of the Mediterranean there should be centers for resting, youth camps, sanatoria, dispensaries. A vast construction project should be initiated for the purpose of rest and relaxation. The whole of the south should be an unbroken series of sanatoria, resting homes for the industrial north, for people of any nationality. For all nationalities. A unified, uniform economic, legal and political space will create favorable conditions for the development of all arts and crafts, for culture, for education, life, in such a way as to satisfy the wishes of all."[1]

Zhirinovsky does not suggest the execution of such a plan along, say, the shores of the Caspian Sea: that would not be any good; no one would believe that such a plan could be realized there. His audience prefers to hear about some impossible project so long as it is outside the area Russia already possesses, as if he were saying, "There, away in far-off lands that we will occupy, everything will be possible." So long as they do it at other people's expense. He also outlines plans for the local population of such occupied areas: where there is a dense concentration of people they can retain their customs, and part of the population will anyway live on the

[1] *The Last Dash to the South*, Moscow, 1993, p. 66.

steppes, in the mountains, in the desert, in yurts, nomadic tents . . . they will tend their cattle; that is quite normal, he says. This plan, however, would soon send shivers down the spines of Estonians, Latvians or Lithuanians, many thousands of whom were indeed made to live on the steppes of Central Asia, where they were deported after the occupation of the Baltic states by Stalin in 1940. But to Zhirinovsky's Russian followers all that would seem reasonable. These things are due to the Russians; they have endured enough. "We have suffered enough. We should make other people suffer," said Zhirinovsky, clearly expecting, and probably getting, approval from his listeners.

It is a culture of self-pity, in which a vast capacity of individuals for warm, human sympathy toward others can turn back toward the feeling subject if he is outraged by what he regards as a bad hand dealt to him or his people by cruel fate. The anger turns outward: a man killing others while being sorry for himself. But the Russian people are "full of mutually contradictory properties,"[2] says Berdyaev: despotism, the hypertrophy of the state and, on the other hand, anarchism and license; cruelty, a disposition to violence and, again, kindliness, humanity and gentleness; a belief in rites and ceremonies, but also a quest for truth; individualism, a heightened consciousness of personality, together with an impersonal collectivism; nationalism, laudation of the self and universalism, the ideal of the universal man; an eschatological messianic spirit of religion, and a devotion that finds its expression in externals; a search for God and a militant godlessness; humility and arrogance; slavery and revolt. But never has Russia been bourgeois.

Also, they can give many things to those peoples that come under their sway, who should really be grateful for it all. Russians, probably more than most colonizers, expect to be loved. As Russian troops were withdrawn from Central European countries in the Warsaw Pact, on the day of their departure many soldiers had flowers in their

[2] N. Berdyaev, *The Russian Idea* (reprint), Greenwood Press, Westport, Conn., 1979.

hands, hoping for a warm "adieu," and were hurt when hardly anybody turned up at the railway stations, and those who did come seemed to be in a different frame of mind. Russians are sincerely hurt that they are not wanted in the Baltic states, for instance. It may be a feeling of unrequited love, in response to which Zhirinovsky has made many harsh statements about the former republics (see Chapter 1). It is partly that, but also they feel that they spent, or rather wasted, a lot of money on these republics—helped them to Russia's own detriment. An important point of Zhirinovsky's program for the rehabilitation of the Russian economy is to stop providing former satellites with fuel and raw materials and, of course, all kinds of aid, so they will come crawling back (see Chapter 1 and Chapter 5). It is quite true that in Soviet times some Western and Caucasian republics had a higher standard of living than the Russian Federation, and the same was true of some Central European countries under Russian occupation. The Soviets did not benefit all that much from their colonies, failing to turn expansion to their profit, but at the same time they greatly hampered the economic development of these countries and republics. To judge by the words of Zhirinovsky, that will and readiness to make sacrifices for the sake of expansion is still there; it has survived another break in Russian history. Perhaps he hopes that next time it will turn out differently—a novel application of Dr. Johnson's "triumph of hope over experience."

In any case, Zhirinovsky feels that Russia can bring peace and order to turbulent areas. That was, in fact, the case in Soviet times, and it was recognized by some people in the West too. In 1957 Carew Hunt, an Oxford don, by no means a left-winger, remarked to an East European: "After all, the part of the world you come from caused two world wars, and now the Russians have taken it out of circulation. Shouldn't we be grateful?" That opinion may be echoed nowadays given the crisis in the former Yugoslavia. An opportunity for Russian peace-keeping forces in Bosnia has already opened up. Zhirinovsky has certainly anticipated such a role for some time: "I have an idea for . . . using armies abroad . . . soldiers under contract for hard currency could serve and perform tasks assigned by the world community," he said in an interview given to *Krasnaya Zvezda* in May 1991.

It can be argued that Russia's vastness and propinquity to every chief geopolitical zone of the world, Europe, the Middle East, the Far East and North America, has been Russia's curse. Not on island continents, as are the USA and Australia, it has to be worried about attacks from all quarters. Expansion into its vast abode has been the guiding dynamic of Russian history. Whenever it has a Time of Troubles (see Introduction to Chapter 5), with a loss of land, its immediate reaction afterward has been to take it back and expand even farther. By extending its power across the globe, even into Africa and fatally into Afghanistan, the USSR came unstuck.

Zhirinovsky's irredentist call to expand is just the latest in Russia's history, in its new Time of Troubles. What looks antiquated and nineteenth-century to the West or Japan seems normal, a matter of common sense, to Zhirinovsky and his followers.

The singular lack of success in making Russia "the richest country in the world" instead of being "downright beggars" has given rise to two attitudes in many Russians: self-pity, sometimes bordering on despair, and an ever-present suspicion that they are victims of evil plots hatched either inside Russia or abroad.

PLOTS GALORE

Xenophobia in General and Anti-Semitism in Particular

As for internal enemies, the first on the list are the Jews. Anti-Semitism is, of course, far from being a monopoly of Russians, but it is said to permeate particularly deeply present-day Russian society. It has straddled the "interruptions" that are "characteristic of Russian history."[3] In the twentieth century, for example, tsarist Russia's problems have been blamed on it, just as has Communism, which, according to prevalent opinion, was foisted on Russia by "Marx and the Jewish Bolsheviks: Lenin(!), Trotsky, etc." The same applies to the current economic reforms ("the Jewish Gaidar"), which have been causing so much misery. Anti-Semitic rhetoric is therefore an absolute necessity for a populist demagogue. It is poignant that Zhirinovsky himself is half-Jewish, which he resolutely, though rather ineffectually, denies. The question is, did so many people vote for him despite that fact, or in ignorance of it, in the December 1993 elections? That is a question we do not feel qualified to answer, but if they supported him despite his having a Jewish lineage on his father's side, could it be that they think, "There is our chance. We have a clever Jew on our side; he will surely be able to sort out those Jewish plotters, and he will know how to get hold of the secret of becoming a rich country, which those Westerners discuss at their G7 meetings, to which no Russian can gain entry"? It must, however, be said that Zhirinovsky condemns Hitler for marring national socialism with racism (see Chapter 6).

As for conspiracy theory—another widespread feeling in many countries—it gains special meaning through Russian military might. One hundred years ago the Russian philosopher Vladimir Solovev wrote the following:

> Let us imagine a person healthy in body and strong, talented and not unkind—for such is, quite justly, the general view of the Russian people. We know that this person (or people) is now in a very sorry state. If we want to help him, we have first to understand what is wrong with him. Thus we learn that he is not really mad; his mind is merely afflicted to a considerable extent by false ideas approaching *folie de grandeur* and a hostility toward everyone and everything. Indifferent to his

[3] Berdyaev, *The Russian Idea.*

real advantage, indifferent to the damage likely to be caused, he imagines dangers that do not exist and builds upon this the most absurd propositions. It seems to him that all his neighbors offend him, that they insufficiently bow to his greatness and in every way want to harm him. He accuses everyone in his family of damaging and deserting him, of crossing over to the enemy camp. He imagines that his neighbors want to undermine his house and even to launch an armed attack. Therefore he will spend enormous sums on the purchase of guns, revolvers and iron locks. If he has any time left, he will turn against his family.[4]

Added to this is the Russian feeling that—like the Serbs—Russians win wars and lose the peace. Zhirinovsky's bellicose rhetoric can hardly come as a surprise. In fact, any nationalist politician is likely to be "afflicted" by the same sentiment. And nationalism—a pendant of the xenophobic conspiracy theory—is hardly to be avoided in the difficult times Russia is now going through.

The Vote of the Dead

One of the arguments G. K. Chesterton advanced—half tongue in cheek, no doubt—in defense of conservatism was that a real democracy cannot rely exclusively on the opinion of the people who happen to be alive at any particular time; the vote of dead forebears must equally be taken into account. In the case of fanatical nationalism the dead are enfranchised to help form a mythical public opinion, and the democracy embracing the dead is trusted to flourish. Is that, perhaps, the role of the word "democratic" in the name of Zhirinovsky's party?

[4] Quoted in Walter Laqueur, *Black Hundred*, HarperCollins, New York, 1993.

The Latest Avatar

Zhirinovsky's racism and xenophobia are amply illustrated in Chapter 6; they are of the usual kind, so they need little explanation. The only aspect of his stance that jars is that he does not want even Jews to leave Russia on the grounds that Russia has always been a multi-national society and it should remain so (see Chapter 6), although he adds that ideally a nation should consist of only one nationality.

The main external enemy for Zhirinovsky is the West because anti-Western feeling is quickly spreading in Russia (see Chapter 6). He has to ride this wave and can also use it for demonstrating his opposition to the present government, even though its "market romanticism" is quickly fading.

ANTI-WESTERN ATTITUDES

Hostility to the West has a long and venerable history in Russia, although it has been punctuated by sometimes quite long periods when at least some sections of the society have succumbed to the blandishments of well-organized and intellectually sophisticated Western countries.

The oldest objection is a religious one, the opposition of the Orthodox Church to Rome, which has weathered all historical changes and is periodically revived through its association with Russian nationalism or with the Orthodox brotherhood idea. An example of this is the present Russian–Serb axis (see Chapter 3).

A different but also fairly consistent anti-Western theme is that many Russians recoil from Western rationalism; on the theological plane medieval scholasticism was always considered spiritually barren and antagonistic to Orthodoxy and, later, to the "Russian idea." Intellectualism is pernicious for the "Russian soul." As Tyuchev put it: "Russia is not to be understood by intellectual processes. You cannot take her measurements with a common yardstick. She has a form and a stature of her own: you can only believe in Russia."[5]

The periodic Westernizing tendencies of Russian rulers provided a rich source of anti-Western feeling. The reforms of Peter the Great, who had traveled extensively in Europe and saw the necessity of introducing fundamental changes in Russia, not least by modernizing the Russian army and navy, marked a century of Westernization; it was only skin-deep, but both he and, later, Catherine the Great were so resolute in that policy, their "snobbery" toward the West was so profound, that it gave rise to a typically Russian phenomenon, which was later very skillfully adapted by the Bolsheviks to their own scheme of things.

The Potemkin Village Effect

Potemkin villages were façade villages constructed out of stage décor, which passed, at a distance, for real villages; with them Catherine the Great wanted to impress her foreign visitors. Prince Gregory Potemkin, who was her lover and one of her ministers, invented the idea. He suggested to the Empress that its implementation would be appropriate for the occasion of the visit of Emperor Joseph II of Austria and the Polish king, Stanislaw Poniatowski, to southern Russia in 1787.

Catherine attempted and succeeded in the creation of a court around herself in which German and French writers and philosophers gathered and raised the intellectual level of St. Petersburg. Catherine was a German princess who knew exactly what Western courts were like. She also knew that St. Petersburg, despite its architectural splendor, was not the result of organic evolution, as it would have been in a much more evenly developed European country, but an artificial implant by her predecessor in an essentially very backward country. The Empress wanted to use Potemkin villages in an extended, metaphorical sense as well, to suffuse her entire reign

[5] Quoted by Berdyaev, *The Russian Idea*, p. 1.

with an aura of enlightened despotism. Eminent foreign visitors and admirers like Diderot, Euler and Voltaire praised her rule and held her up as an example to be emulated. In fact, her reign saw the greatest peasant revolt of Russian history, that of Pugachev in 1773–4, which was a revolt against the harsher terms of serfdom imposed by Catherine herself.

The construction of Potemkin villages did not continue after Catherine the Great, but the concept of pretense systems had already taken root in the country and, in that conceptual sense, was used extensively at later times in Russian history, in particular that of the most ambitious, impossibly ambitious, project Moscow ever had—that of the Bolsheviks, who not only wanted to catch up with Western countries and equal them in both military strength and social and political eminence but also aimed at leading the world in the construction of an entirely new society, in which Western countries, mere acolytes, would sedulously imitate the Russian example.

Communist society turned out to be even more repressive than Russian society was under the tsars. Under Stalin the population was subjected to atrocious conditions, mentally as well as physically; the threat of arrest and deportation to Siberia loomed constantly.

In the countries of Western Europe, however, some people took seriously Stalin's and his successors' pretense that the Soviet Union was a completely new and model country. The Communist Parties followed Moscow's lead, and one after another Western intellectuals visited the Soviet Union from the 1930s to as late as the 1970s, were taken in by the Potemkin façade created for their benefit by the Soviet authorities through carefully arranged tours of a few new model cities and their shops, listened to the opinions of "the ordinary people" stage-set for them by the KGB, then came back knowing nothing about the archipelago of labor camps all over the country and extolled the new Soviet regime. Among them in the 1930s was G. B. Shaw, who was not even a Communist, only an idealist. He also took the word for the deed, the façade for the real thing. Many other Western intellectuals were prepared to project the few model

"Potemkin" towns and industrial centers, shops and "ordinary people" on to the whole country.[6] Even later, after Khrushchev's revelations about Stalin and the brutal repression of the Hungarian revolution in 1956, though some Western Communists were disillusioned, other left-wingers, anticipating Gorbachev, suggested that the Soviet Union might need some time to develop fully but was on the right path and would eventually eliminate all shortcomings and establish "Communism with a human face."

The greatest success of the Potemkin effect, however, was yet to come—when some leaders of the Soviet Union, cocooned in their closed *nomenklatura* world, started to believe their own rhetoric and thought that they could reform the Soviet Union and create that "Communism with a human face," notably Mikhail Gorbachev who, overpowered by his own Western snobbery, in the end went through the door of a theoretical Potemkin façade, tried to sit down on a state-of-the-art Potemkin hologram-chair and fell to the real ground.

Another example of Bolshevik Potemkin construction was the creation of the republics, thereby sometimes fostering the separate national identity of, for instance, the Kazakhs, the Turkmens, the Kyrghyz. The Russians wanted to give the impression that Communism was already international and was going to include an ever-growing number of countries—the Communist messianic message made that necessary. Little did the Bolsheviks suspect that this pretense would one day come home to roost. But the majority of Russians, even if they are not very interested in the issue, are convinced that most of the former republics are integral parts of Russia and should remain so.

The Potemkin image lives on; at the end of the Brezhnev epoch a Russian woman, on her first trip to the West, walked along the Kurfürstendamm in West Berlin and exclaimed: "But this is a Potemkin village! You can't all be this rich!"

---

[6] See P. Hollander, *Political Pilgrims*, Oxford University Press, New York, 1981.

How would Zhirinovsky's Potemkin world come about? Is it that he pretends to be the long-suffering little man who has endured so much humiliation and hardship behind the façade (see Chapter 6)? Or is his game to call the Potemkin bluff of some of the reformers?

AN IMPOSSIBLE-PROJECT SYNDROME

Russian history has been studded with a long series of impossible projects; enthused by their vast and rich land, the Russians have long believed that they should be the natural rulers of the world. This view is aptly reflected in a deduction made by the English geopolitician Sir Halford Mackinder, of which Zhirinovsky would approve: "He who commands the marches commands the heartland. He who commands the heartland commands the world island. He who commands the world island commands the world."[7]

In the sixteenth century Ivan the Terrible aimed to set up a totalitarian state *avant la lettre* with a secret police force, the *Oprichnina* or 6,000 black horsemen, the elimination of opposed forces and the total control of society, including the restriction of the population to one place. Lacking the means of surveillance to succeed, his rule led to the Time of Troubles (1603–14), when anarchy arose and people wandered around in an unruly way.

A century later Peter the Great tried to Westernize the country and in part succeeded (see introduction to Chapter 5). But he provoked a reaction by the Slavophiles, who cleaved to an idealized image of the Slav union in the past, the very antithesis of the West.

In the eighteenth century Catherine the Great had foreign-policy successes, notably the conquest of most of Poland and the capture of Crimea from the Ottoman Turks. The latter achievement inspired Potemkin to conceive of the Greek Project, which was no less than

[7] Sir Halford Mackinder, *On the Scope and Methods of Geography*, Royal Geographical Society, London, 1951.

the reconstitution of Byzantium as an independent Christian state after the conquest of the Ottoman Empire, based on a renewed Constantinople. Catherine's second grandson was named Constantine in expectation of his ruling there. He was entrusted to a Greek nurse; Catherine ordered medals to be struck with a reproduction of St. Sophia.[8] Her last minister, Zuboff, added India to Turkey as another objective of this push south. Nothing came of it at the time, but it has perhaps inspired Zhirinovsky's conception of the Last Dash to the South.

The nineteenth century saw more reasonable projects adopted and serious economic development begun by its end. But the good prospects ended with 1914. The Bolsheviks at first put in place the aim of igniting revolutions for Communism in the West. When these expectations failed Stalin adopted the goal of making the Soviet Union the lodestar of the whole world, which Moscow was to lead to the promised land of Communism. A *Salvator Mundi* project with a vengeance, the military costs involved in maintaining the Cold War with the West from 1941 onward eventually broke it apart in 1989–91.

But meanwhile Stalin had at least achieved one earlier unfulfilled project, that of Ivan the Terrible. For modern technology now allowed the construction of a totalitarian state, complete with *Gulag*, purges and witch trials. As Stalin told N. K. Cherkakov, the actor who played Ivan the Terrible in Eisenstein's film of the same name, the secret police, *Oprichnina*, was a "progressive" idea. Ivan's mistake, in Stalin's view, was not to pursue his purges far enough.[9] This was not an error Stalin could be accused of making.

Indeed, it was revulsion against the Stalinist record that led Gorbachev to his idea of Communism with a human face, of *glasnost* and *perestroika*. This proved to be another impossible Russian proj-

[8] Nikolai Riasanovsky, A *History of Russia* (4th edition), OUP, 1984, p. 266.
[9] Paul Dukes, A *History of Russia, Medieval, Modern and Contemporary*, Macmillan, 1974, p. 53.

ect, as the Chinese have duly noted. One can have *glasnost* or *perestroika*, but not both together. The former leads to the collapse of Communism forthwith, the latter to its delayed collapse while saving one's face.

THE SOUL PITTED AGAINST LUXURY PLASTIC

Peter the Great tried to Westernize Russia, which by reaction induced Slavophilism and the conservation of the "Great Russian soul," the very antithesis of the West. Even St. Petersburg, his dazzling new capital, the Venice of the North, was built not organically, like Venice, but with Asiatic brutality on a swamp, killing nearly a million forced laborers from among the serfs. Catherine the Great understood that it was wiser to refrain from action in this regard and that it was better simply to talk and to pretend.

Contemporary Anti-Westernism

The nineteenth-century debate between pro-Western and anti-Western parties continued until the First World War, but with the victory of the Bolsheviks no further debate was possible. The staunch anti-Western stance of the Communists, however, gradually promoted pro-Western attitudes, as an ever-increasing number of people lost their hope in any substantial change, and finally, from the late 1960s onward, the leadership became more and more cynical and society more and more corrupt (see below, "Mafia Capitalism").

With Gorbachev at the helm of the party, pro-Western attitudes became respectable, but at the same time the old debate between Russophiles and Westerners started up again. The prestige of the West rose in many people's eyes; much hope was pinned on Western help. The West gave the impression of knowing how to help Russia to its feet after the collapse of Communism. Western experts went in droves, set norms for the reforms and tied aid to the achievement of certain targets. The IMF and the World Bank were confident about their advice. Professor Sachs of Harvard University was appointed economic adviser to the reformist government, which now follows fewer and fewer of his suggestions. The Russian government has lost its trust in Western experts—or perhaps its nerve in the face of the increasing dissatisfaction.

Robert Ericson, head of the Harriman Institute at Columbia University, New York, thinks that the entire conception of the IMF and the World Bank of how to rescue Russia from the consequences of Communism and create a free-market economy is misconceived. In *The Bear Contained*, BBC Radio 4, 24.3.94, he quoted an old Russian saying about Communism: "Building Communism was like taking an aquarium and making fish soup of it," adding that rebuilding capitalism from Communism might be "like taking the fish soup and trying to reconstitute the aquarium."

The old economy started to decline fast; the development of the new was not able to keep pace with it; problems of livelihood overshadowed everything in everybody's mind—and what do human rights and democracy mean to those who have hardly anything to eat and no fuel to keep them warm through the long, bitterly cold Russian winter? Most people were lost in that new world, where they had no idea how to go about things, what to do, how to join in a "new" society and how to conform to new practices.

The Soviet regime was bad, but most people knew their place. Everybody knew what he or she could do and what not; everybody was monitored; and practically the only way up was through the Communist Party. Stepping out of line was quickly punished, and justice was arbitrary. The people were treated like minors, whose father was the Party: a bad father, no doubt, a nasty, shabby drunkard who beat its children, but still a father. Salaries were very low, but at that very low level there was financial security for everybody. With a bit on the side (see below, "Low-level Corruption"), most people eked out an existence.

With the Communist regime suddenly gone, everybody was free

to act, but most people are still completely lost in this new world, where they have to behave as adults and take decisions formerly taken by others for them but do not know how to go about it: having got rid of their drunkard father, they have become orphans. Disillusionment, bewilderment and fear of the future are growing, just as is fear of the present as the streets have become more and more violent, ruled by gangs.

With the Soviet Union, the latest avatar of the Russian messianic empire, gone, national identity was shaken, for even in the Brezhnev days of corrupt stagnation there was some ambient pride left in being a top republic among the other fourteen and a superpower in the world.

Western help was not forthcoming at the rate, and in the way, people had expected. Many people began to suspect that the West, and especially the USA, just wanted to have Russia running after it, without really having any hope of catching up. They found the role of the little lap dog, faithfully trailing its master, humiliating. The West does, indeed, like its economic and social superiority seasoned by moral superiority: only if its advice is followed will the pupil be rewarded. That has already caused resentment in many countries; Islamic fundamentalism, for instance, feeds off that resentment in part. Many nations, especially ones with a long history and a rich culture, know that they have values that the West lacks, and they want to preserve them and pit them against the inferior spiritual values, as they see them, of the West. Iran is a case in point, as are many other Islamic countries. Russians are proud of their soul and their emotional depth. They may admire and even envy the West but feel that people in the West are not quite real people: there is nothing much behind that polished exterior; they seem to be made of plastic, their existence an ontological anomaly; they seem empty strutting through their boutiquified cities, within the corrals of their pedestrian precincts—haughty but lost souls.

"There is that in the Russian soul which corresponds to the immensity, the vagueness, the infinitude of the Russian land; spiritual geography corresponds with physical. In the Russian soul there is a sort of immensity, a vagueness, a predilection for the infinite," says Berdyaev, "such as is suggested by the great plain of Russia. For this reason the Russian people have found difficulty in achieving mastery over these vast expanses and in reducing them to orderly shape. There has been a vast elemental strength in the Russian people combined with a comparatively weak sense of form."[10] Berdyaev speaks of a phenomenon germane to Dostoyevsky's *gestaltlose Weite*, formless distances unfettered, undefined by form, as being real Christianity.[11] And now the Russians have to face up to the rigors of modernity: all shape and form, no internal space or yawning depth of the soul. All that counts is the unblemished, hard enamel of the surface.

Enter the Savior

Then comes a strange little man. They call him a buffoon both in the West and in Russian reformist circles (although the latest Moscow stance is that he is mad, a clinical case, perhaps a wistful reflection of the good old Soviet days when dissidents could be locked up in psychiatric hospitals). He claims that he, like everybody else, suffered in childhood, and he makes extravagant promises to restore public order, reoccupy the republics, double the standard of living in a couple of months and lead the Russians to a monstrous Torremolinos stretching for thousands of miles along the northern shores of the Gulf of Oman and of the Arabian Sea, as Russian soldiers with handy small but efficient automatic weapons watch over the peace of the exhausted northerners.

The poor lumpenized masses are his constituency, and he is proud of it. He banks on the further degradation of the population and

[10] Berdyaev, *The Russian Idea*.
[11] Carl Schmitt, *Romische Katholizismus und Politische Form*, Klett-Cotta, Stuttgart, 1984, p. 55.

makes no secret of it; and his stock has been appreciating considerably in the past eighteen months.

In October 1992 an interview with him was published in the *New Times International*, in which he flaunted his brazen "lumpeno-philia." The interviewer told him: "It is very easy to make such extravagant promises to people. There is an enormous lumpenized mass which will buy them." Zhirinovsky: "It will buy them all right." Interviewer: "But, after all, the nation is not composed of lumpens alone. Lots of people retain common sense." Zhirinovsky: "They do. They vote against, but they will be in the minority." Interviewer: "So far they are in a substantial majority. Do you reckon on the degradation of the masses?" Zhirinovsky: "I most certainly do!"[12]

He has pitted himself against everybody: the remnants of the old *nomenklatura*, the "*nomenklatura* kids" among the reformers, the sleek, new Russian businessmen, the merciless *mafiosniki* and the implacable extreme right wing, way beyond him.

ON THE WINGS OF THE RUSSIAN RIGHT

If Zhirinovsky knew Lewis Carroll's *Through the Looking Glass*, he might, when told that he was a right-wing extremist, adopt the logic of the Red Queen and retort: "You may call me a right-wing extremist, but I could show you right-wingers in Russia in comparison with whom I am the most stolid of moderates."

In Pamyat circles—Pamyat is an ultra-nationalist, far-right group—Zhirinovsky is quite beyond the pale but not because of his extremism; on the contrary, he is seen as a dubious cheat, a traitor, the agent of a global conspiracy against the rebirth of Russia and against God the Almighty. And as a nationalist he is quite unsatisfactory because he took part in parliamentary elections, which shows that he thinks in Western terms. Election anyway is a manifestation of

[12] *New Times International*, October 1992, p.11.

leveling decadence. Moreover, his father was a Jew; so no right-wing extremist of the Pamyat stamp worth his salt would ever want to be seen rubbing shoulders with him. Dimitri Vasilyev, the head of Pamyat, is a staunch monarchist and wants the tsar back but will have nothing to do with any descendant of the Romanovs in Western Europe because their stock is no longer pure. Many decades of intermarriage have rendered them unsuitable for the task: a new dynasty must be found. And he rejects Nazism on the ground that it was born on the rubbish heap of Bolshevism.[13]

Fascist groups even further to the right are, for instance, the street bands of Alexander Barkashov, which concentrate entirely on violence.

All present-day conservative nationalist movements hark back in some way or other to their common ancestor, the Black Hundred, who, as Walter Laqueur explains, "are a unique phenomenon in the history of twentieth-century politics, as it was a halfway house between the old-fashioned reactionary movements of the nineteenth century and the right-wing populist (Fascist) parties of the twentieth. With their strong ties to monarchy and Church they largely belonged to the past, but unlike the early conservative groups they were no longer élitist."[14] They had come to assume their new role during the crisis of tsarism in 1904–5. He speaks about "them" because the Black Hundred was not a single organization but a "somewhat catch-all term for various extreme right-wing groups that existed between, roughly speaking, the turn of the century and 1917," explains Walter Laqueur. With the coming to power of the Bolsheviks the right went underground but was not entirely eliminated. Their ideas maintained their clandestine existence in the Soviet Union and were pursued openly by Russian emigrants abroad.

After the "fall" of Trotsky and the indefinite postponement of "world revolution" Stalin decided to make do with "socialism in one

[13] *Der Spiegel*, No. 8, 1994.
[14] Laqueur, *Black Hundred*.

country"; consequently the Soviet Union became increasingly national socialist and eventually was as nationalist as Russia had been under the tsars; Russian nationalism was subsumed under Communism and the subterranean circulation of most right-wing ideas continued in that new packaging. That is why there had come to be such a strong Communist element in the new Russian right as it gradually emerged in the Gorbachev years.

All through the Soviet period the façade of internationalism was carefully maintained, but Russian nationalism was an additive in practically all Soviet policies and measures. A new Potemkin village was added to the existing stock. The successive Communist Party leaders varied as to the emphasis they laid on the internationalist epidermis or on the underlying Russian nationalism bone structure. The promotion of regional ethnic development in the republics continued on the surface—the Soviet leadership was quite confident that it would never get out of hand and could not weaken Moscow's hold over the republics. The local ethnic groups, however, were not deceived by the surface internationalism: they were experiencing the very strong nationalist strain in Moscow's rule all the time. Their hostility to it may well have contributed later to sometimes precipitate declarations of independence as well as to the self-assertion of one republic against another—in the Caucasus, for instance. Regional ethnic-nationalist ideas had also been "firmed up" in their opposition to Russian chauvinism in the Soviet period. A very strong Russian nationalism was equally experienced in the Communist satellite countries of Eastern Europe. Without this Russian imperialist chauvinism, Communism as such might have gained marginally more support. Outside observers, say in the West, were often oblivious of what became a very important factor later, at the end of the Gorbachev era, and has remained so since the collapse of the Soviet Union.

Both Soviet ideology and the Black Hundred–type thought were strongly anti-liberal and anti-Western, which facilitated a "tacit agreement" between them. The Soviet leadership probably noticed the further alienation of the nationalities and the ethnic groups in the republics and in the autonomous republics of the Russian federation respectively but were confident that it could be contained (as Khrushchev clearly thought that the inclusion of the Crimea in the Ukraine would spell no danger to the Russians living there).

As Walter Laqueur explains: "Three centuries of Russian history were undone in a few days in August 1991 as the result of the weakness of the center. To save the remnant, a spiritual as well as a political renaissance is needed, a return to the national and religious values of the Russian people. It is pointless to embrace Western values and to copy Western institutions. Russia had always followed a road of its own; political systems that functioned elsewhere were unsuitable for Russia."[15]

As the new Russian right emerged under Gorbachev's *glasnost* it was carrying with it a sizable Communist load, which it had taken on during seven decades. Its anti-Semitism survived unscathed the long years spent under the mask of anti-Zionism. Conspiracy paranoia was a strong feature of Stalinism, and it was congruent with the same tendency later in the right-wing movements as they came out of hibernation. Therefore it is not surprising that parts of the "patriotic intelligentsia" allied itself with some of the KGB and of the high military command as well as with the staunch remnants of the ex-Soviet leadership in August 1991. That community of minds makes it also quite easy for pro-Soviet militants to switch to militant nationalism as the need arises.

The so-called red-brown elements straddle the two ends of the scale, so to speak, and will perhaps help the serpent to bite its own tail. Such a man is Alexander Prokhanov, geopolitical novelist and editor of the militant paper *Zavtra*, formerly *Dyen* (the latter was banned after the defeat of the armed parliamentary revolt in October 1993 because of its closeness to the Rutskoy cause). The resurgent *Eurasianism*, pleading for a Eurasian-Russian Great Empire, finds

[15] Laqueur, *Black Hundred*, p. ix.

new supporters every day. Nikita Michalkov, the internationally well-known film producer, for instance, has given up being Yeltsin's adviser on cultural policy and has turned against the Western reforms and the Western concept of liberty in favor of Eurasianism.

Conservative (that is, Communist) elements around Rutskoy find it easy to mingle with the born-again Russian extreme nationalists, and ex–Red Army militants will probably be able to mix easily with resurgent Cossacks to follow one or another aspiring right-wing leader. The distribution of the forces thus generated will probably determine, to some extent at least, whether a new future political crisis will flare up into a civil war, how bitter it will be and, from the point of view of this book, how Zhirinovsky will fare in this struggle for survival of the fittest.

THE REFORMERS

The latest impossible project for Russia is to try to turn it into a liberal-democrat and consumer-capitalist country in a few years or one generation at the most. This was precisely the aim of first the Yavlinsky "500-day" plan for capitalism, which Gorbachev toyed with but then dropped, and then the Gaidar reform team's "shock therapy" plan.

Shock therapy is the traditional IMF medicine for a developing or developed country in a crisis with over-swollen state spending and inflation. Cutting back the state sector and curtailing monetary growth can then bring down inflation and allow resources to switch to the private sector.

The trouble with this in Russia is that it is neither a developing nor a developed country but a profoundly misdeveloped one. After seventy years of Communism, with the ruination of its agriculture by forced collectivization in the 1930s and a bloated military–industrial complex, shock therapy does not right the financial economy by much, but it does derange the real economy, which is collapsing as a consequence.

Basically, the very infrastructure in Russia was misdeveloped—the oil and gas pipelines are rusty and leak, the roads are pockmarked, the airplanes of Aeroflot are unsafe to fly—while the environment is the most polluted in the world and partially radioactive to boot (fifty mini-reactors of a Chernobyl type were put within Greater Moscow, causing the distribution of radioactive dust all over the city). Of the numerous conditions needing to be met for a successful take-off into capitalist growth, Russia has but a few—an educated workforce, good scientists and engineers and access to abundant resources and energy—but the legal, fiscal and, above all, cultural contexts of capitalism are quite lacking.

People are hostile to private property, says Russian film maker Andrei Konchalovsky. "In Russia people despise wealth. Just look at the way private farmers who strike out on their own are the subject of hostility from everyone else."[16] This attitude, indeed, explains why the expropriation of the *kulaks*, the better-off farmers of tsarist Russia and the 1920s New Economic Policy, was possible in the 1930s, the lesser peasants and the policemen involved scorning them for being well-off. Such attitudes lead to rich farmers facing arson of their lofts or farm buildings and theft of their equipment and livestock. "People here almost consciously reject the idea that they can be rich if they work hard," Konchalovsky says, adding that illogical tax laws nobody could afford to obey (demanding up to 85 percent of turnover for the taxman) could only encourage lying, cheating and bribery. "Russians seem to prefer to be poor."[17]

Such attitudes date from the tsarist epoch and are hard to eradicate. The reform team of Yegor Gaidar and his men, Boris Fyodorov and Anatoly Chubais (still in power as head of the privatization process, the one reform still going on), allowed a brief reign of

[16] *The Sunday Times*, 1 May 1994, p. 23.
[17] *The Sunday Times*, 1 May 1994, p. 23.

macroeconomic policy from December 1991 to December 1992, when Victor Chernonyrdin, an old-style industrialist and head of Gasprom, took over from Gaidar as premier.

Chernomyrdin calls himself a reformer too—as do all Russian politicians except the Communists and ultra-nationalists. In fact, Chernomyrdin was keen to appoint a fellow Soviet *apparatchik*, Victor Gerashchenko, to the key post of head of the Russian Central Bank in July 1992. The new boss did a U-turn and began to issue credits to the state firms that the Gaidar team had cut. As controller of the distribution of credit, Gerashchenko is in a position to assume, in an economy become "privatized" and subject to market forces, the role of the old Gosplan Five-year-planners in charge of the distribution of resources: the credit confers purchasing power in the market for those very resources.

Gerashchenko justifies his liberal use of credit by a novel argument: claiming to be no less monetarist than the Gaidar team, he does not deny the fact that there is a link between money changes and prices changes, postulated by the Quantity Theory of Money. He thinks that it is only of a different character than usually thought. Money increases, far from stimulating price rises, stimulate production and so enable demand to be satisfied more easily, thereby countering inflation. This is veritably monetarism *à la Russe*.

The aim, of course, has been to keep Russian workers in work by ensuring a flow of finance to their employers and so preventing Zhirinovosky from coming to power. But one cannot use *Alice in Wonderland* economics to avert *Through the Looking Glass* (darkly) geopolitics. Printing money to chase goods, mostly at the wrong times of production, means hyper-inflation in the prices of those goods people want.

Gaidar made a comeback in April 1993 as deputy premier for reform. He was able to force a measure of financial discipline on the Russian Central Bank by means of advocacy from younger, reform-minded bankers so that Russian inflation fell from over 20 percent per month in early 1993 to under 10 percent for a while in early 1994. But the sharp cuts in credit to state firms meant that his influence was greatly resented by them and he lost his job, as did his ally, Boris Fyodorov, Minister of Finance, after the December 1993 election.

A return to Gerashchenko-economics took place for a while in early 1994, leading to expectations of a resurgence in inflation by 1993 unless the bank's chairman's wings are clipped by Chernomyrdin.

Gaidar, Fyodorov and Chernomyrdin are not really feared by Zhirinovosky because they have all been tried and have visibly failed. The one reformer with an unblemished reputation is Gregory Yavlinsky, whose Center for Economic and Social Research has prepared a report on economic reform for the Nizhni Novgovorod region, whose governor, Boris Nemtsev, is a physicist-turned-reformer and is pioneering a grass-roots reform, privatizing farms with foreign help and pushing for new industries out of defense conversion. It shows the LDPR's (Liberal Democratic Party of Russia) appeal that, even so, it obtained 18 percent of the vote there in the December 1993 election.

Yavlinsky is, then, the one serious centrist candidate for the presidency, explicitly opposed to the rapid brand of reform applied so far and with a fresh-faced appeal to many voters, who, however, never taps the groundswell of nationalism stirring in Russia as Zhirinovsky incomparably does.

MAFIA CAPITALISM

The Soviet Union under Stalin established law and order on the streets in its own way. Gangsters were put in the GULAG, where they often became guards. By a curious paradox every subsequent Soviet or Russian leader has unwittingly, except possibly in Brezhnev's case, encouraged the rise of gangsterism. Khrushchev released from the GULAG the "thieves elders," as they are called, who formed gangs engaged in the usual repertoire of drugs, gambling and prostitution.

In Brezhnev's time a new generation of gangsters emerged that exploited the shadow economy that was springing up in the interstices of the command administrative system. It became common for moonlighting firms to operate businesses with the bribed connivance of daytime bosses, using state materials to produce goods for the black market. This was doubly illegal because it was misappropriating state assets and because capitalism of any sort was banned. Such shadow businesses were hence good targets for mafia-type extortionists.

Perestroika and *glasnost* were a new boon to the gangsters, who were able to strengthen their international links. The Caucasus peoples, especially the Azeri, the Chechen and the Georgian and Tambov gangs, provided many of the leading *mafiosi* of Moscow and the main towns. Dealing in arms, caviar and "out of legal hours" alcohol, one of their most profitable lines was drugs from Central Asia sold in the West. Uzbekistan has 3,000 poppy fields, and Kazakhstan is a world leader in cannabis production. In Tajikistan opium and cannabis have replaced dollars as the side currency. Italian and Russian mobsters planned to have 40 percent of the world's drug traffic under their control by 1992.

A further extension of the mafia's activity into armaments was made possible by the break-up of much of the Red Army and yet again by Gorbachev's prohibition of alcohol from 1986 onwards. Prohibition ruined many fine vineyards but did not stop the production of vodka, which carried on in the black economy. "As soon as the state . . . let the reins drop and lost control of vodka, political troubles inevitably followed. Problems that had earlier been hidden emerged into the open."[18]

Prophetic words—for by 1992 the USSR had ceased to exist and the Russian and Caucasian mafia gangs began to go legitimate in

[18] Andrei Pokhlebkin, A *History of Vodka*, Verso, 1991, p. 175.

certain activities in the rapidly spreading private economy. Komsomol holiday camps became training grounds for contract killers recruited from the disintegrating army.[19] Extortion of other private firms under threat of contract murder became common. Some 90 percent of the private sector is now under mafia control;[20] some 40 percent of the existing Russian economy is also.[21] The banking sector has been targeted. Ten senior bankers were killed in 1993 for failing to extend further "loans," while Moscow's senior grandfather himself and a Duma member were gunned down in April 1994. The murder rate has reached Lebanese proportions, which, with inter-gang killings and contract murder, is twenty-five times the UK rate.[22]

The chaos associated with *perestroika* allowed tens of thousands of corrupt factories and trading firms to team up with the big mafia and sell billions of dollars' worth of Russia's precious materials, mostly from the Baltic states and ports, notably St. Petersburg, but also from the Black Sea ports and the Far East. In 1988 scrap-metal exports became legal when Russian technology could not reprocess it. This loophole has been fully exploited. The mafia has also diversified into scrap-metal export and energy, a third of whose exports are estimated to be contraband. Through forgeries and bribes for police and customs officials they began to sell copper, zinc, aluminum and other strategic materials in vast amounts, keeping the proceeds in the West for fear of a clean-up campaign at home.[23]

There are now between 3,000 and 5,000 gangs operating right across Russia from St. Petersburg to Vladivostock, two cities of intense mafia activity. Racketeering, like prostitution, was deemed not to exist in the Communist paradise, and neither is illegal. But even smugglers and those held on murder charges often get off, since 70

[19] *Daily Mail*, 19 March 1993.
[20] *Focus*, January 1994, p. 44.
[21] *The Sunday Times*, 1 May 1994, p. 7.
[22] *Focus*, January 1994, p. 42.
[23] *Newsweek*, 5 October 1992, p. 18.

percent of the police force is corrupt. One policeman in St. Petersburg apparently refused a US$700,000 bribe to be turned.[24] Where one refused, how many would accept?

St. Petersburg has only a twenty-four-man squad, with deficient facilities, to tackle the mafia, where 5,000 is the minimum needed. Mayor Anatoly Sobchak has called for the Defense Ministry to take over the task, but it refuses, saying that Interior Ministry troops should do so.[25] Zhirinvosky wants a special task force, recruited from the army and carefully vetted, to take up the job, with results expected within three months or the top man loses his job. This approach is what is required, indeed, and is the most popular policy he advocates. If he could be seen to tackle at least the small-fry *mafiosi* hitting the kiosks, shops and restaurants, between 70 and 80 percent of which pay 10–20 percent of their earnings as extortion, according to a special report commissioned by Yeltsin, then a Zhirinovsky presidency would immediately enhance its appeal. The big-time mafia fleecing of the nation's resources would be harder to stop, but a dictatorship such as Zhirinovsky advocates, with 100,000 being shot within three months, is probably the only way a dent could be made here. Mussolini cleaned up Italy in a brutal way.

The Russian attitude to private wealth has always been a troubled one, regarding it as sinful, although there are some 7,000 dollar millionaires in Russia. This attitude, to which film maker Andrei Konchalovsky ascribes much of his country's woes, he captures thus: "In Russia, the more wealthy a man is, the further he is from God, so when you steal from him you are bringing him closer to God."[26] Soulful gangsters dispense salvation along with extortion and mayhem!

The scale of the mafia fleecing of Russia is shown by figures collected by the Institute of International Finance (IIF), the world

[24] *Newsweek*, 5 October 1992, p. 18.
[25] The *Independent*, 3 May 1994, p. 10.
[26] *The Sunday Times*, 1 May 1994, p. 23.

banking community's think-tank. The IIF estimates that US$90 billion has been earned by Russians selling materials and energy to the West since 1991, of which US$40 billion has not been repatriated.[27] A further source of profit is the printing by rogue elements in the KGB's successor agency of counterfeit currency, especially US dollars. Some US$10 billion–$15,000 billion is circulating in Russia illegally, according to the head of the regulations department of the Russian Central Bank, Viktor Melnikov, a sum greater than the total value of rubles in circulation.[28] Many of these dollars must come from counterfeit sources.

The outward-bound direction of the Russian mafia is making Western police uneasy, since the intention is to engage in similar activities in, say, Germany, the UK and the USA. Toughened by survival in a totalitarian state, it is convinced that it is far more ruthless than local mobs—indeed, is matchless. In a sinister echo of Khrushchev's "We'll bury you" threat, one Russian gangster says: "We'll overwhelm you. We'll overwhelm you and your neighbors in the common European home."[29] The West cannot be said not to have been warned. If Zhirinovsky comes to power and wages a campaign against the mafia, this could accelerate its exodus to the West, much as tightening in Italy is leading to Italian mafia migration abroad.

LOW-LEVEL CORRUPTION

Corruption in Soviet society spread far beyond the *mafiosi* and the criminal rings. It involved a large section, probably the majority, of

[27] *Financial Times*, 19 April 1994, p. 2.
[28] Russian TV channel, 20 April 1994. Mr. Melnikov is reported by BBC Monitoring, Caversham, as saying US$10–$15 million, but this is contradicted by the next clause and must have been a mishearing. That Russian dollars are over US$10 billion is attested by IMF officials independently.
[29] *Focus*, January 1994, p. 48.

the population. Such activities, though illegal, were in the domain of socially acceptable illegality.

There were three basic kinds. You could expect payment or gifts for services, the provision of which was part of your job. A nurse in a hospital could expect payment for performing her ordinary duties, such as giving meals to patients (or at least giving reasonable meals to patients), a doctor for treating a patient in a health service that was supposed to be free. But the doctor himself had to pay a laboratory assistant for a routine blood test done for a patient of his in the hospital, for instance.

Domestic repairs that were supposed to be provided free by a housing-estate management were not done, or at least not done properly, unless every time the workman was given some extra money, which meant an income over and above his salary.

What did those people do who were not in a service profession but worked in a factory? They had the opportunity of stealing materials, tools, etc., from the factory and either using them or selling them. Or they could use the factory equipment for producing articles that they could sell privately. In agriculture state farm workers could sell privately produce that was the property of the state.

As people were generally badly paid, even though the necessities were inexpensive—basic foodstuffs, transport, homes and average clothing—a very large number of people did not find it easy to make ends meet if they wanted anything above the absolutely basic. The slightest luxury was far beyond their means. And what they were able to afford made for a very drab life indeed.

(Zhirinovsky complains in his writings and in his speeches, perhaps insincerely, about the poverty he suffered as a child: he had no toys, no books, had to eat the bad canteen food that his mother brought back from work. He hopes to give the impression that he has shared the general hardship of the ordinary Russian citizen and that this will bring him closer to his potential constituency.)

An illegal income was not considered criminal: it was generally accepted, but it still meant a frail public morality. From the higher echelons of an illicit income the jump to the lowest grade of actual criminality was not great. And nobody considered stealing state property a real crime when done on a small scale, nor the system of taking small bribes. The state itself was seen as a racket of some sort, run by a very small circle of privileged people. And the frail public morality proved fertile ground for "development" when the walls of the Soviet structure began to crumble, for those who were ready.

All in all, ways of getting extra cash involved a very high percentage of the working population—probably well over half of them. Those in positions of power had, of course, the best opportunities.

RULER AS CLOWN

The reason why Zhirinovsky is considered unlikely to become president by many in Russia and the West is that he is a clown, a court jester. There is, however, a long tradition of the buffoon in Russian politics, upon which he is drawing.

During the Soviet period the tradition was banned, although Khrushchev quite consciously, and Brezhnev unconsciously, had their decidedly clownish sides. Khrushchev banged the table at the UN with his shoe to make a point—country-bumpkin behavior that contributed to his downfall. But his successor developed his own absurdities, conferring on himself literary awards for unreadable tomes that accumulated unread on the book shelves, while overloading his chest with medals for supposed deeds in the Great Patriotic War, in which he and his cronies turned the tide. A whole culture of political jokes emerged to lampoon him and his corrupt court. But, whatever they did, they kept on the whole to the leaden Soviet style of public speaking.

Zhirinovsky breaks with all that dramatically. The more outlandish his utterances, the more he distances himself from the Soviet times and associates himself with the tsarist world. In Peter the Great's time there was the day of the fools, 1 April, when the jester with his cap and bells was king.

Zhirinovsky is flaunting his Russian soulfulness with his rages and antics, such as pelting Jewish demonstrators from the Russian legation in Strasbourg in March 1993. He is expressing his contempt for the West and all its decorum of hypocrisy. Undignified and boorish he may be, but he is for real, the epitome of everything that Communism tried to expunge in the Russian character. Far from hurting him electorally, his clowning is a help—a comic diversion for the Russians in their desperation and a reminder of the absurdity of their situation and of life.

An anecdote that can, perhaps, drive this home is told by Christabel Bielenberg, a British woman married to a German lawyer from Hamburg who was a liberal opposed to the Nazi regime. In late 1932 they attended a Nazi meeting out of curiosity to find out about the phenomenon. Halfway through Hitler's speech Bielenberg jacked his future wife out of the crowd and said loudly, within earshot of the organizers: "You may think that Germans are political idiots, Chris, and you may be right. But of one thing I can assure you: they won't be so stupid as to fall for *that* clown."[30] Three months later Hitler became Chancellor of Germany.

[30] Christabel Bielenberg, *The Past Is Myself*, Corgi Books, 1984, p. 22.

Absolute Zhirinovsky

The Near-Abroad or Former Soviet Union Outside Russia

A RÉSUMÉ OF RUSSIAN IMPERIALISM

Zhirinovsky evinces a great respect for history—before 1914. He seems to think that only if a country was independent before then has it a right to exist today. Hence the importance of establishing Russia's acquisitions before this crucial watershed. It is these territories that he has in his sights in an imagined recreation of the empire of the tsars, a fantasy he would like to turn into a reality. The Russian state has always been an expansionist one. Its original home around Kiev in the tenth century was under one three-hundredth of its present extent. In 1462 it covered 15,000 square miles. By 1914 it occupied 8,660,000 square miles, the ethnic Russians establishing dominion over more than a hundred very different nationalities.[1]

Expansion was several times punctuated by a "Time of Troubles," in 1603–14, 1917–20 and, most spectacularly, 1989, with massive relinquishment of territory. But Russia has already begun to expand

---

[1] *Russian Imperialism from Ivan the Terrible to the Revolution*, ed. Taras Hunczak, Rutgers University Press, 1974, Foreword, p. 1.

again, now into Abkhazia, prised from Georgia, and it is re-establishing control over Tajikistan and Belarus.

Russian imperialism has been not just a practical matter of self-defense and self-assertion, the peasant habit of coveting that extra strip of territory, but also a messianic affair. "Messianic consciousness is more characteristic of the Russians than of any other people except the Jews. It runs all through Russian history down to the Communist period."[2] After the fall of Constantinople in 1453, Russia assumed the leadership of Orthodoxy and became the Third Rome with the mission to lead the faithful. "The Russian religious vocation is linked with the power and transcendent majesty of the Russian state, with a distinctive significance and importance attached to the Russian tsar. There enters into the messianic consciousness the alluring temptation of imperialism."[3]

It is estimated that Russia was adding 50 square miles per day to its territory for four centuries before 1914. This encroachment came as a series of responses to outside invasion, such as that of the Tartars, Germans, Poles and Swedes. New territory was seized for security reasons. But then this territory required its own security zone. Adding security zone to security zone, Russia expanded to its natural limits, the Baltic, the Arctic, the Pacific Ocean, the Altai, the Pamirs, the Causasus and the Carpathian mountains. Even then the expansionist habit led to the acquisition of Alaska, Finland and, southward beyond the northern Caucasus range, Georgia, Armenia and Azerbaijan.

The Expansion of the Tsarist Empire

After Ivan the Terrible had taken the last Tartar strongholds in the east (the Crimean was not incorporated until 1783, Kazan in 1552 and Astrakhan in 1556), the way was clear for expansion to Siberia.

---

[2] Nicholas Berdyaev, *The Russian Idea*, Greenwood Press, 1979 (reprint), p. 8.
[3] Berdyaev, *The Russian Idea*, p. 9.

The Cossacks, under their heroic leader Yermak, went around the Urals in 1581. By 1649 the Russians had reached as far as the Pacific rim.

Russia experienced a grave "Time of Troubles" in 1603–14, when its territorial integrity was severely shaken. But as usual in Russian history, trouble prompted the Russians to expand, and a Cossack rebellion in Ukraine enabled this ancient heart of Rus to be rejoined with Russia in 1654. Peter the Great acquired Estonia, Livonia (part of modern Latvia), the mouth of the Neva, on which he built St. Petersburg, and part of Karelia from the Swedes by 1721. Catherine the Great seized Crimea in 1783, subjugating the Crimean Tartars who had previously owed allegiance to the Ottoman Sultan, and gained the Black Sea coast by the Dnieper by 1792 in fighting back the Ottoman Turks.

To the west Russia obtained the lion's share of Poland under Catherine in three partitions of the country, carried out with Prussia and Habsburg Austria, in 1772, 1793 and 1795. The 1793 gains brought the bulk of White Russia (now Belarus) to rejoin its eastern areas already in Russia, after having been Polish for centuries, while the 1795 acquisition brought into the empire Lithuania, which had also been in Poland since the Union of Lublin in 1569.

In 1809 Finland was taken from Sweden, after a successful one-year campaign against the Swedes, and incorporated in the empire as an autonomous Grand Duchy, the tsar being its Grand Duke. The Finns cooperated with the Russians in quelling repeated Polish revolt, but they were to resent the Russian yoke as much as the Poles when a misguided policy of Russification began in the 1890s. Pushing southwards across the northern Caucasian mountains, Russia took Georgia by stages in 1801–10 and Daghestan and northern Azerbaijan in the same decade, occasioning a successful war with the Turks and Persians, who recognized Russian sovereignty by 1813. As a result of the war Russia was in a position to straddle the entire Caucasus range, taking Armenia by 1828, although a famous Muslim rebellion in Azerbaijan under the legendary Imam Shamil did not die out until the early 1860s.

In the West, after repelling Napoleon in 1811–12 the Russians occupied Bessarabia in 1812, which, with part of Moldavia taken in 1829, forms the core of modern Moldova. After acquiring Alaska in 1799, the Russians erected Fort Ross in northern California.

In a long process of piecemeal absorption the Kirghiz steppe was incorporated in the empire from 1731 to 1734, bringing areas of modern Kazakhstan and Uzbekistan and Turkmenistan under Russian tutelage. They were not fully acquired until 1865–76, when conquest of the khanates of Kokand, Bokhara and Khiva brought the whole of Central Asia, including Kyrgyzstan and Tajikistan, under the tsar. This was done to prompt interference in the region by the British, pushing up from India into Afghanistan, and as a compensation for the sale of Alaska to the United States in 1867, for only US$7,200,000. Indeed, the Great Game between Russia and Britain in Central Asia set the pattern for subsequent geopolitical rivalries across the Eurasian continent, notably the Cold War (1946–89). Turkey and Persia were great players in the game then. The Russians justified seizure of Central Asia on the ground that they would save the people there from tribal disunity and dismemberment at the hands of Turkey and Persia, though it is not recorded if the Central Asians themselves appreciated Russia's public spirit in this regard.[4]

In 1847 the energetic Count Nicholas Muraviev, known later as Muravyev-Amyursky (that is, of the Amur) became the Governor General of eastern Siberia. He promoted Russian advance in the Amur and secured gains from China, which was beset by war with Britain and France and by internal rebellion. In 1858 China ceded the left bank of the Amur and, in 1860, the Ussuri region. The Pacific coast began to be settled, the town of Nikolaevsk on the Amur being founded in 1853, Khabarovsk in 1858 and Vladivostok ("Ruler of the East") in 1860. In 1875 Russia yielded the Kuril islands to

[4] Nicholas Ch. Riyazanovsky, A *History of Russia*, 4th edition, OUP, 1984, p. 390.

Japan in exchange for the southern half of the island of Sakhalin,[5] which, however, it was to be forced to relinquish to Japan after losing the 1905 war to it. The Trans-Siberian railway, begun in 1891, was supposed to commence the integration of the vast empire as one common economic space. By the 1880s the tsarist empire reached its zenith, including one sixth of the land area of the globe, until then the largest territorially contiguous empire in history.

The Shattering of the Tsarist Empire and its Supersession by the Soviet Union

The First World War gave this vast structure a terrible battering, which proved fatal by 1917. The Soviet Union emerged in its wake. The Bolsheviks had to give up Poland (not without a fight), the Baltic States, Finland and Bessarabia, which rejoined an enlarged Romania in 1918–19. Ukraine, White Russia, the Transcaucasus Federation (to be dissolved into the separate states of Azerbaijan, Armenia and Georgia) and Central Asia broke away with independence movements. But after winning the Civil War of 1918–20 the Soviets reimposed Russian control over them by 1924, with the Georgian Stalin, the connoisseur Commissar for nationalists, urging and executing a Great Russian chauvinist policy. This time it was not the supposed benefits of benign autocracy that were invoked to justify Russian rule but the blessings of the international fraternity of workers and peasants uniting in their own state. Proletarian solidarity was the ideological carapace of the Soviet state and could justify indefinite extension beyond Russia's geographical limits.

In 1939 Stalin made a pact with Hitler that enabled him in June 1940 to incorporate the Baltic states and Bessarabia, which with Trans-Dniestra constituted the Soviet Moldovan Republic or what is modern Moldova. In 1945 victory in the Second World War enabled

[5] Paul Dykes, A History of Russia, Medieval, Modern and Contemporary, 2nd edition, Macmillan, 1990, p. 140.

the Soviet Empire to extend "from Stettin in the Baltic to Trieste in the Adriatic," to use Churchill's graphic phrase in his "Iron Curtain" speech at Fulton in 1946, marking the onset of the Cold War. Even after the loss of Tito's Yugoslavia in 1948, the Soviet Empire in Central Europe incorporated over 100 million people, living in Eastern Germany, Poland, Czechoslovakia, Hungary, Bulgaria and Romania (which asserted a certain independence by the 1960s under Ceauçescu). In the guise of socialist brotherhood, Moscow by then ruled an empire of 400 million over a vast expanse of territory, nearly one fifth of the world's land area, eclipsing even the tsarist empire as the largest territorially contiguous empire of history.

The New "Time of Troubles"

The events of 1989–91 were traumatic for the Russians. First in 1989 Central Europe broke away, as country after country had a liberal and nationalist revolution. Then the USSR itself cracked open in 1990, as Lithuania declared its independence, and finally dissolved in August–December 1991, as one Soviet republic after another declared its independence. The 25 million Russians living in the Near-Abroad became justifiably apprehensive. From being colonial masters they became at best second-class citizens in the non-Russian republics, and often, as in the Baltic states, not citizens at all unless they could pass stringent language and residency tests. By 1993–4, after experiencing harassment and economic misery, the 7 million Russians in Kazakhstan, mostly in the north, and the 11 million in Ukraine, mostly in the east, began to cast longing looks at Russia, desiring their reincorporation—which in turn makes Kazakhs and Ukrainians apprehensive about Russian intentions. Some Russians have been returning, but enough remain to cause inter-ethnic tensions. This astonishing collapse has left the Russians stunned and in disarray, particularly as their command state economy is sliding into chaos as well. A "Time of Troubles" is upon them with a vengeance. The question remains whether Russia can keep itself together with *de facto* independence emerging in its outer regions, such as the Russian Far East, Daghestan and the other north Caucasus republics. Yet the urge to expand has already reasserted itself. Abkhazia, with Russian troop support, has gone independent from Georgia, and its formally western province of Georgia has returned to the Russian fold in all but name. Tajikistan and Belarus have been brought under economic and military control; Azerbaijan, north Kazakhstan and east Ukraine are also coming within the ultra-nationalist sights. Zhirinovsky's rhetoric seems to offer a further extension of Russia's borders to the historic frontiers of 1914, with even Alaska added as a fine flourish. The ardent desire for extra land, the Russian geopolitical obsession *par excellence*, is renewing itself in Zhirinovsky, who echoes the saga of centuries of endless expansion.

THE GENERAL CONCEPTION OF THE NEAR-ABROAD

The concept of the Near-Abroad was made up by the Russians immediately after the collapse of the Soviet Union in order to distinguish the newly independent republics from other independent countries of long standing around them. Clearly, it affords less status and, because virtually everybody in Russia considers these republics integral parts of Russia, it may bode ill for the independence of these new states. Neither the British nor the Americans use the expression "Near-Abroad" officially; they want to avoid getting into the invidious position—in the event of Russia reoccupying, say, the Baltic states—of having in any way condoned such an action.

On 13 December 1993, the very day news was coming through of a stunning electoral victory for the LDPR, the text of an interview with its leader on Serbian TV, Belgrade, was published. An interviewer, Jasmina Stamenić-Pavlović, asked Zhirinovsky: "What are your party's main slogans?" He replied: **Over a year ago we took a moderate stance regarding all issues, of a rightist-center patriotic orientation. We are against the restoration of the USSR; we are** against the CIS; we favor the restoration of the Russian state as a homeland for all. That is the formula we believe in. National divisions imply constant war, constant friction, constant border issues, accusations, retaliation; of course, all of this is unacceptable. To create new states today, at the end of the twentieth century, that is too expensive and tragic. (Serbian TV, Belgrade, 13.12.93)

We must force our republics to return. How? And we should not be good-natured toward them. Kindness is a wonderful quality in a human being, but it's bad for the state. We buy from Uzbekistan third-rate cotton at world prices. We should trade in this way: in exchange for your crappy cotton, we will give you two Zhigulis [small cars] and goodbye. They'll starve—then let them starve. Tribal societies should starve. Why should they be sated at the expense of our civilized Russian nation? (*Kuranty*, 16.11.93)

An interviewer for *Izvestiya* accused Zhirinovsky of publicly proposing the restoration of the tsarist empire by war, abolishing the republics of the Near-Abroad and turning them into provinces ruled by Russian government generals. There will be no war. All these territories—the Baltics, Bessarabia, Caucasus—historically belong to Russia. I proceed from the beginning of history, and you from the end. We need not conquer them. Everything is very simple. We have only to stop supplying timber to Ukraine and all mines of the Donbass are bound to collapse. If we stop supplying everything which we currently supply to Ukraine, the Kravchuk government will crumble in three months. Stop aid, including military aid, to Tajikistan and you'll have Rakhmonov fleeing to Moscow and begging, "Admit us as a Russian province." (*Izvestiya*, 30.11.93)

As for ex-Soviet states, Russia supported and fed them under the Communists. Ukraine was the only one to manage it alone, and with great difficulty . . . Stop helping them, and they won't last a

8

month. Why should we inflict suffering upon ourselves? Let's make others suffer. (*Izvestiya*, 30.1.93)

We Russians have helped all the republics much too much; we have built everything for them. And since everything we put there is being destroyed, we do not want to help them any more. (*Die Zeit*, 4.2.94)

The flow of refugees [Russians returning from the republics that have become independent] is easy to stop; if we threaten the regions from where Russians are driven out with doing the same thing to their indigenous people in Russia, that will suffice.

Take, for instance Azerbaijan. Of 500,000 Russians who lived there a mere 100,000 remain. Now, how many Azeris are hanging about Russia at present? One million. So for a start we must evict 400,000 Azeris from Russia to Baku and tell them that if they dare bully Russians again, we'll give back the whole million. The same applies to other regions. Don't forget that there is no democracy without violence. (*Izvestiya*, 30.11.93)

We must all become citizens of Russia. But by Russia I understand the whole of the territory of our state, from the Baltic to the Pacific, from Kushka to Murmansk and from Kishinev to Kamchatka. So I'd like us to return to the old name of our state. Then it would be clear what we were talking about . . . As a lawyer, I regard the 1977 Constitution as valid in this country. Under the Constitution, we have existing external state borders, and the Baltic Republics, *inter alia*, are part of our country. (Soviet Television, 31.5.91)

Ex-Soviet Union republics, Georgia, Azerbaijan, Armenia or the Central Asian republics—they want to be included in Russia. We don't want that because there's no profit to be together. (Oesterreich 1 Radio, Vienna, 22.12.93)

I am against even a single meter of Soviet territory coming under the jurisdiction of an alien, foreign flag. I should therefore like to see questions of sovereignty resolved in the economic sphere. Economic sovereignty, economic power only, should be given to all regions, oblasts and republics, so that they—to put it in down-to-earth language—choke on that power and ask the center to take back a part of it. That is the model that is needed—not to reject claims by regions and territories for economic powers but, on the contrary, to give them as many as possible. (Soviet Television, 22.5.91)

I want to tell you bluntly whose side I'd take; in Georgia I will be defending the interests of the Abkhaz people and the Osetians. In the quarrel between Azerbaijan and Armenia I will tell you bluntly that I'd take the Armenian side.

The Russian president must have a clear-cut position on all these problems. Then the peoples of Russia and the whole of the USSR will calm down. Today, when there is anarchy, when power is paralyzed and when the economy and culture have disintegrated, civil war is effectively on our ethnic periphery, and our state continues to disintegrate. (Soviet Television, 22.5.91)

Russia's soldiers will once more stand guard over the 1975 border of the Soviet Union, and once we have put them there, they will not move back a single step. (*Financial Times*, 14.12.93)

The republics wanted independence; they'll beg us on their knees to let them belong to Russia. We will make them provinces. (*La Stampa*, 16.12.93)

The frontiers of the USSR as of 1975, recognized by the world community, will be restored and Russian flags will fly over the cities of Kazakhstan, Central Asia, the Transcaucasus, etc. (ITAR-TASS, World Service Radio, 2.4.94)

Imperialism and colonial policy are foreign notions. We have no such things here. It was normal for us to have colonies. It was good, it was right. (*New Times International*, February 1992)

I will introduce an economic blockade to force the Baltic region to return to Russia. I would use the military as a means to solve the problem of Kazakhstan. Against the Ukraine I would use some military means and some economic measure. (Interview with Zhirinovsky, *Aftenposten*, Oslo, 4.11.91)

I'll bury nuclear waste along the border. I'll move the Semipalatinsk test site to your area. You Lithuanians will die from diseases and radiation. (*Time*, 17.2.94)

Moldova and the Baltic republics will be reduced to the size of Liechtenstein, and the Ukraine must give us back the whole of its southern and eastern regions. (*Frankfurter Allgemeine*, 16.12.93 quoted from *The Last Dash to the South*)

As a possible future president of Russia I want to raise the Russian issue, not because I want the Russian nation to lord it again, but because we have raised all the ethnic issues as they relate to all regions but have forgotten about the Russian people—155 million Russians whom nobody needs!

They find themselves in a particularly sorry plight in the national republics—25 million Russians there have become second-class citizens. For this reason I should very much like to see the new president of Russia be not only president of Russia but also president for all Russians living on the territory of the USSR and all Russian speakers and to take under his protection all the small peoples. (Soviet Television, 22.5.91)

Here one cannot fail to speak about the ethnic question and the state borders. When I spoke on Friday [19 November, 1993] some people said: "The Baltics and Moldova are far away; I live in the Urals and as a pensioner I want a normal, calm life." But you are not going to live a quiet and calm life in the Urals or in Magadan if we do not have normal borders.

For example, all of us together built Novotallinsky port [Estonia] under the Communists; it cost 4 billion roubles. It is no longer ours. Now we are building another port, in Leningrad Oblast—more billions of our money. So you pensioners are not going to live better if we are going to lose territories, ports, roads, communications, the southern regions where it is warmer and better. We are all linked together. (Russia TV Channel, Moscow, 23.11.93)

Just look who has suffered most today. Again, it is pensioners of Russian nationality. Why? Well, the Baltics are trying to avoid pensions. Or take the Transcaucasus or Central Asia. They have lost more than anyone. Or take servicemen. They have served their term and are now outside the borders of Russia. Not only can they not receive their service pension, but they are not allowed into any form of activity, since they served, allegedly, in an army of occupation.

To prevent this, to prevent millions of our fellow citizens suddenly, at the end of their lives, from becoming occupationists or colonists, we must have a correct state policy. If people such as Travkin [head of a neo-Fascist party, the Democratic Party of Russia] have a good knowledge of how to build pigsties, we have great need of this. But the State Duma will not be building pigsties. It will be building a new Russian state. And here, experience in building pigsties is not applicable; it is terrible. (Russia TV Channel, Moscow, 23.11.93).

With the change of leadership in Russia, many non-professional politicians got into political life. They are considered amateurs by those who oppose them. On the other hand, they are clean of mistakes made during the Soviet regime.

SLAVIC REPUBLICS AND MOLDOVA

President Mircea Snegur of Moldova recalled in mid-December 1993 that in pre-election speeches Zhirinovsky had made covetous remarks about his republic.

The Republic of Moldova is none other than a province of Russia with an already-appointed governor—the commander of the 14th Russian Army stationed in Tiraspol. (*Commersant Daily*, 15.12.93)

Tiraspol is the capital of Trans-Dnestr, a Russian military base on the left bank of the river Dnestr, the rest of the republic being on the river's right bank. The commander of the 14th Army is General Alexander Lebed, a strong supporter of Zhirinovsky's party.

Moldova [alongside the Baltic Republics] **will be reduced to the size of Liechtenstein.** (*Frankfurter Allgemeine*, 16.13.93)

In answer to the question "How can Russia get Ukraine back?": **It is all quite simple. We will stop deliveries of timber to Ukraine and all the mines of the Donbass will collapse. In fact, we will stop supplying anything: in three months the Ukrainians will be on their knees begging us to take them back.** (*Frankfurter Allgemeine*, 14.12.93)

Ukraine must give us back the whole of the eastern and southern parts. (*Frankfurter Allgemeine*, 16.12.93)

Russia will not feed Ukraine as western Germany feeds eastern Germany (*Die Zeit*, 4.2.94)

Zhirinovsky said of Nikita Khrushchev, the former First Secretary of the Communist Party, that he **was to blame for the loss of Crimea, which had been developed at the expense of all the people** (Russia TV Channel, Moscow, 23.11.93). Khruschchev, who was the First

Secretary of the Ukrainian Communist Party in the 1940s, handed over the Crimea to Ukraine in 1954. To him this must have seemed a wholly formal procedure without any possible consequences; little did he know. It is now, of course, a highly contentious issue with Russia, since the majority of the population there is, in fact, Russian, and they do not want to belong to Ukraine—it may even become the cause of a war between the two states.

According to Zhirinovsky, President Yeltsin paid 1 billion roubles in fuel for the Black Sea fleet. His comment on that: **I will take the money from them both for the fuel and for the fleet** (*Die Zeit*, 4.2.94)

The map on which he redrew the frontiers in Central and Eastern Europe shows the annexation of the Baltic states and of Moldavia, Ukraine and Belarus. As for Russian expansion to the south, he affirms in his book that **reaching the Indian Ocean is vitally important for the Russian nation, on which depends its survival.**

THE BALTIC STATES

On Western ambassadors to the Baltic republics, which he intends to abolish: **They are going to leave the same way they came.** (*The American Spectator*, March 1992)

Lithuania will understand this [the strength of the union] **through economics. Give them an opportunity to separate, but only in the 1940 borders. But who in Europe will buy Lithuanian cheese? We need it, but there no one does . . . The other way is back to the union. Who, for example, will reconcile the Chechen and the Ingush? Only a Russian governor.** (Interview with Zhirinovsky, *Leningradskaya Pravda*, 25.6.91)

In the autumn of 1991 Zhirinovsky asked the Baltfax correspondent to inform the three Baltic state presidents of the time, Landsbergis, Gorbunovs and Ruutel, that he was very displeased with them. **Tell them that when I become president of the confederation next spring, they will have to pack their bags. I shall establish a Baltic province. I will have a governor in Riga who will rule Estonia, Latvia and Lithuania.** (Russia's Radio, 5.9.91)

Latvia should belong to Russia. Lithuania will become a small independent state, an enclave. (*Die Welt*, 29.1.94).

Instead of the three Baltic republics, there will be one province headed by Governor-general Alksnis. (TASS, 8.7.91) Colonel Alksnis from Latvia is a prominent advocate of the restoration of the Soviet Union and supported the August *coup* plotters in 1991 one month after Zhirinovsky made this statement.

The Baltic republics will be reduced to the size of Liechtenstein. (*Frankfurter Allgemeine*, 16.12.93)

I love the Balts. We would gladly live together [with the Balts]. **All problems can be settled. God save us from hatred.**

[The Balts] **are a nice, cultured nation. And you need us. We won't build any frontiers, and Russians would gladly learn Estonian and Lithuanian if only the most favorable solution can be reached.**

Lithuania would speak Russian, Polish and Lithuanian; Estonia would speak Estonian and Russian; and Kaliningrad could speak Russian and German. Just as in Finland, where people use both Finnish and Swedish. And [interethnic] **relations are normal there.**

I say I love the Balts. I have a slightly negative attitude toward the southerners [presumably the former Soviet southern republics] **because there are too many criminals among them.**

But our party cherishes the warmest feelings toward the Baltics. It was the journalists who portrayed us as enemies of the Baltic

states. I met **Landsbergis** [former Lithuanian Supreme Council chairman] **and I met representatives of the Latvian Supreme Council. I tried to call Arnold Ruutel** [former Estonian Supreme Council chairman] **in January 1991, but he was busy. I was everywhere, in Tallinn, in Parnu, in Riga—I was everywhere, and I know everything.**

We have the best attitude toward the Baltics. I say, I love you all, Estonians, Latvians and Lithuanians, and all Russians who live there. The Baltics is a region of the highest culture and the broadest cooperation—no soldiers, no shooting, mere economy, culture and festivals. (BNS, Tallinn, 14.12.93)

Zhirinovsky was then asked if he was ready to speak to the Baltics in the language of sovereign countries instead of the language of provinces. It's a completely different issue. If Estonians, Latvians and Lithuanians are able to build their countries without discrimination and in compliance with international law, we are ready [to let them do it]. But if they jeer at Russians, depriving them of voting rights, and steal from Russia what belongs to Russia, then we will be forced to use defensive means.

As economists and lawyers, we understand that the Baltics have the cold Baltic Sea to their west and Russia to their east. You have only two options; to sail to Sweden or to live at peace with Russia, but the peace must be just. You should not steal from Russia. If you steal, we will try to prevent it. If you try to deprive Russians of their rights, we will respond with such steps that you will have no electors left to stage elections. For we will always support any Russian, Pole or German who has Russian citizenship. If you use force to deprive them of voting rights, evict them from apartments, dismiss them from jobs, we will use economic methods only to square all accounts with the Baltics, and your countries will collapse two weeks after I have become the president of Russia. There will not be a single Baltic country if you continue your thievish policies. (BNS, Tallinn, 14.12.93)

This irredentist position began to influence Russian foreign policy very soon after the LDPR's stunning victory in mid-December 1993. The Russians had agreed to withdraw the 10,000 troops they had in Latvia and the 3,500 troops in Estonia by August of 1994; this was confirmed at the US–Russian summit in early January 1994.

Then on 18 January 1994 Mr. Andrei Kozyrev, the Russian Foreign Minister, indicated that Russian troops would stay in the Baltic in spite of these commitments. He told a conference on Russian policy toward the countries of the CIS and the Baltic states that complete withdrawal of troops "from this region" would be against Russia's interest because it would create a security vacuum and would leave local ethnic Russians undefended. "We should not withdraw from these regions which have been in the sphere of Russian interests for centuries, and we should not fear these words," TASS quoted him as saying. His confidence expressing the words is obviously attributable to the wild words on the same and kindred subjects uttered by Zhirinovsky.

Estonia: **If they don't behave, we'll switch off their lights.** (*La Stampa*, 16.12.93)

When I speak about closing borders to whom do I mean this should apply? Only to those who rob us. We and you Russians will have total freedom. You will be able to move in any direction. But some sections of the border—say, the Caucasus—could be made stronger or even closed.

In the Baltic there should be tight customs crossings. At present they are growing rich by stealing our non-ferrous metals, timber and so on. At the same time their living standards are getting worse and worse.

They have more and more suicides. In Estonia, where Russians are deprived of electoral rights, where they have no incomes and there are many unemployed, the number of suicides is greater among Estonians. That is proof of the viability of the Russian

nation, of the fact that it is more resilient and that it is not a colonizer.

In the free Estonia of today the Estonians are doing away with themselves. They cannot stand it; they are ashamed that Estonia and other independent states are living on the proceeds of robbing and thieving from Russia. Only after two and a half years were flimsy customs posts finally put up. Money was spent on this. Our money—from your pockets, pensioners. They should have been made to do this—the Estonians, Latvians and Lithuanians. But borders with Russia are not to their advantage. They benefit from open borders. And why? To steal. (Russia TV Channel, Moscow, 23.11.93) Zhirinovsky commented after this that a vote for the LDPR would combat this deplorable problem.

Estonia should be part of Russia, since there are many Russians living there. However, Tallinn should remain a city-state. (*Die Welt*, 29.1.94)

The new Tallinn port cost 4 billion roubles. And they gave it away as a show of good will. And now we are building our own in Luga, breaking our backs in the process. Meanwhile the Estonians keep stealing. A nation of 900,000 and every one of them is a thief! A nation of thieves!

Politics is the art of deception, and we shouldn't be hindered by this factor. However, while we're good-natured and preen ourselves before world opinion, our people will starve and live in misery. (*Kuranty*, 16.12.93)

The LDPR has a representative in Estonia, Petr Rozhok, who asserts that Estonia continues to be an ancient Russian territory. According to him, neither the peace treaty of Uusikaupunki of 1721, confirming Russian occupation of Estonia, nor the Helsinki Treaty of 1975, also doing so, has been repealed.

The 3,000 Russian troops and tens of thousands of retired Russian servicemen and reservists living in Estonia should know, he says, that they are living in an ancient Russian territory. He has appealed to these servicemen to form defense units. Nevertheless, he has been persuading Zhirinovsky not to use phrases such as "Let us bring our tanks" but to threaten Estonia with economic sanctions only in order to secure its reunion with Russia.

The Estonian government has brought a criminal case against Mr. Rozhok, who has been charged for instigating ethnic hostility. Zhirinovsky promptly, on 9 February 1994, voiced outspoken threats against each and every one of the 900,000 ethnic Estonians (there are 600,000 Russian Estonians in Estonia) if the government proceeded with legal action against his representative in the country. He said: **I warn the Estonian government that if even a hair should fall from the representative of the LDPR, Petr Rozhok, the Estonian government will have to think about the fate of 900,000 Estonians. I'll swap one Rozhok for 900,000 Estonians. If Rozhok is put into an Estonian jail, an end will come to Estonia and Tallinn** [Estonia's capital]. **We will implement such measures that the Estonians will forget that they are Estonians** (BNS, 92.2.94). The premier, Mart Laar, stated on 10 February 1994 that the origins of anti-Jewish leaflets that were being distributed in Estonia must also be investigated. They might have some connection with the LDPR, he claimed.

Mr. Laar said that it would benefit Zhirinovsky to use tranquillizers from time to time: "Zhirinovsky's irritation has set us pleasantly in the company of all those East European nations with which he has already expressed his annoyance." **The Baltics are Russian land. I will destroy you. I will start burying nuclear waste in the border zone of Smolensk Oblast; the Semipalatinsk will be transferred to your area. You Lithuanians will die of disease and radiation. I will remove the Russians and the Poles. I am God. I am a tyrant. There will be no Lithuanians, Latvians or Estonians in the Baltics. I will act like Hitler in 1932. The champagne you are quaffing today is your own wake.** (*National Affairs*, 3.10.91).

It may well be that such wild statements do not make the same horrifying impression on his Russian audience—his sole concern—as they do on us, who are accustomed to euphemisms and extreme verbal circumspection—which does not mean that they do not send a chill down the spines of Lithuanians, of course.

THE CAUCASUS

When a hundred or two hundred years ago the Georgian tsar sent his delegation, Georgia was perishing, awash with blood spilt by alien invaders. This treaty says: with Russia for eternity. It was Georgia that was asking—but today they reject us and today the Transcaucasus military district troops there are occupants. If we were not there, there would have been no Georgia or Armenia on the political map of the world. I say this as an Eastern expert . . . The maps of the general staff of the Iranian and Turkish armies do not feature Georgia—all this is shaded there as provinces, or *vilayets*, of Turkey and Iran. The word "Batumi" is not written there—it is Batum-Kale, Sukhum-Kale and it is because the Soviet troops are there that Georgia and Armenia exist . . . So, let them stop and think about the future of their countries and not strive for independence . . . let Georgia and Armenia die for the edification of all the peoples of the Soviet Union. They will die within a year; these two republics will disappear. It is a matter of great regret for me, but it will happen because they are situated in a region in which they will not be able to stand on their own two feet. (Soviet Television, 22.5.91)

There were no states in the Caucasus; it was just a tract of wilderness (*New Times International*, October 1992). Here Zhirinovsky bends history to his own ideas. The Caucasus in the early nineteenth century, when Russia conquered it, was no tract of wilderness. Of course, he may simply be ignorant of this fact.

When Azerbaijan and Georgia crawl back on their knees, imploring to join Russia, they should be quarantined for as long as possible. (*Izvestiya*, 10.11.1993).

The Caucasus must be cut off from Russia, separated by a Berlin Wall. We must confine ourselves to observation, while selling weapons to all factions. The Caucasus was conquered by Russia and not assimilated—we must never forget that. In the past there were no modern weapons of mass destruction, so the tsar needed the Caucasus as a buffer, as an outpost, but now we have no need for the Caucasus. Let them sort things out between themselves while our diplomats and secret agents keep tabs on them from a distance. (*Le Monde*, 23.12.93)

During the build-up to the December 1993 election Zhirinovsky condemned the Civic Union, a party headed by the chief of the Russian Union of Entrepreneurs and Businessmen. **It appeals for peace, stability and calm, but its leader, Arkady Volsky, is responsible for the ruin of Russia's industry and bloodshed in Nagorno Karabach** (Russia TV Channel, Moscow, 23.11.93).

We don't need to fight . . . We should simply not get involved. They will kill each other: Armenians–Azerbaijanis, Turks–Armenians, mountain peoples–Turks, Afghans–Tajiks, Tajiks–Uzbeks, etc. And then they, or more likely the survivors, will run to beg from Russia some status for district rights (*Kuranty*, 16.12.93). Zhirinovsky's designs southwards take in the Caucasus and Central Asia as one vast stretch of murky, mainly Turkic, disturbance.

Events in the Caucasus demonstrate that, without Russia, civil war breaks out: Armenia against Azerbaijan, Georgia against Abkhazia and Ossetia. The same thing will happen along the southern border of Russia: Uzbeks, Tajiks, Kazakhs—they will all fight one another. There will be no Russian troops in these regions. The only thing we can do is to sell arms. If these peoples want to buy weapons, they can only do it in Russia. We do not want a new Afghanistan. But what do we see there? No government, no president, towns fight against one another, cities get destroyed, the transport breaks down . . . The entire region will perish. Iran, Turkey, Afghanistan will interfere: it'll be an inferno, just like Lebanon or Northern Ireland. Then, twenty or thirty years later, they'll come in tears and beg us . . . Russia could save the situation—chiefly by psychological means . . . Both these regions and the international community will ask us; only if they pay for it will we put an end to the catastrophe—and reliably. (*Die Welt*, 29.1.93)

CENTRAL ASIA

Zhirinovsky has spoken of Uzbekistan, whose capital is Tashkent, as "our Tashkent province." This assault on the republic's independence was attacked in the local press, one Uzbek newspaper saying that his election speech employing the phrase "fell like snow from the sky" (Ostankino Channel 1 TV, Moscow, 26.11.93).

I was born in Central Asia myself, you see. We regard it as Russia, not Central Asia. Initially, it was populated by Russians only, and Russians brought civilization there. The Kazakhs lived in nomad tents. They had no electricity, nothing, and all they had was cattle, sheep breeding. Like all the primitive communal tribes. There was no state there. (*New Times International*, February 1992)

Let Muslim regimes rule in Kabul and in Tashkent. But our government supports the old Communists there. Why? The Komintern again (*Le Monde*, 23.12.93). (For Komintern and Kominternism, see Chapter 6.) At the same time he regards as inevitable Russian domination of Central Asia as well as of the Middle East.

They will all fight among themselves and we will come in when

they invite us (*Guardian*, 31.1.94). That is another piece of wish-projection on the part of Zhirinovsky. His audience, his constituency, is well aware of the danger of civil war in Russia, consequently the dream image he wants to present here is the opposite: a peaceful, and strong Russia that is asked to create order in the turbulent southern regions.

Kazakhstan is an artificial creation that can thrive only under Russian domination. (*Frankfurter Allgemeine*, 16.12.93)

I would ask Mum, "Why do we have such bad housing conditions? Why can't we get an individual apartment?" Mum replied: "We aren't Kazakhs . . . Kazakhs get priority." (*The Last Dash to the South*)

Stop aid, including military aid, to Tajikistan and you'll have Rakhmonov fleeing to Moscow and begging, "Admit us as a Russian province." (*Izvestiya*, 30.11.93)

As a matter of fact, Andrei Kozyrev, Russian Foreign Minister, sounded more bellicose two months earlier than Zhirinovsky was here. Kozyrev, dressed in battle gear in Dushanbe (the Tajik capital), said: "We will not give up Tajikistan without a fight."

TWO

The Security Zone Around the Near-Abroad

Russia has long had grave security concerns, which have intimately shaped its foreign policy and history. Bordering every one of the world's major geopolitical zones, Europe, the Middle East, Central Asia, the Far East and North America, it is keen to pre-empt enemies before they strike, including those from within.

Russian autocracy aimed to establish absolute internal security and external impregnability. Hence Ivan the Terrible's creation, at the discretion of the tsar alone, of what effectively came to be a secret police, the *Oprichnina*, who wore black uniforms and rode on black steeds, foreshadowing the Black Hundred (see Introduction). The Soviet Union aimed at total control over the population by forcing everybody to remain at home by means of the internal passport system; it was a criminal offense, for example, to travel to Moscow without permission, much as serfs in tsarist Russia could not move outside their villages. External security was assured by electric fences, border guards in turrets and pillboxes along thousands of miles of frontier. Foreign visitors were subject to the strictest customs searches and KGB surveillance. An all-enveloping calm was to reign over the Soviet lands.

But the Russians, whether in tsarist or Soviet times, still remained acutely anxious of what lay immediately beyond their borders—hence the idea of security zones to forestall threats lurking therein.

The Russians have been obsessed by conquerors and conspirators against their security for good reasons: the very real attempts made upon them by the Tartars, the Teutonic knights, the Poles, the Swedes, the Ottomans, the French, the British and, in this century, the Japanese in 1905, the Germans in 1914, the British, Americans, French and Japanese in 1918–20, the Japanese again in a little-known war in the Far East in 1936–9, the Nazis in 1941–5 and then the relentless Cold War.

Stalin occupied Central Europe in 1945 to repel and defeat the Nazis. He hung on to it ostensibly to spread the socialist gospel but, more fundamentally, to prevent another Nazi-style invasion. During the Cold War the Soviet Union was surrounded by Western military bases and missiles from Norway to Turkey and Iran, from Korea and Japan to Alaska and the Arctic. When it tried to install missiles in Cuba in 1962, the USA reacted with such hysteria that the Soviet leadership felt all the more strongly. On the other hand, such a reaction was not surprising, since Moscow infringed the not entirely tacit agreement between the two superpowers: the mutual recognition of their respective spheres of influence. The USA accepted Moscow's reassertion of power in its "security zone" in parts of Central Europe by acquiescing in the suppression of the Hungarian revolution by Soviet troops in 1956. The USSR would presumably have been equally hysterical had the Americans done otherwise.

The specter of a profound threat to the Soviet Union appeared in 1979. A fundamentalist Islamic regime came to power in Iran, and since there have always been close ties between Iran and Afghanistan (part of the present area of Afghanistan was historically Iranian land), the possibility that Islamic fundamentalism would spread from Iran was a reasonable assumption to make. The frail pro-Soviet Communist government and ruler was deemed unsafe by

Moscow. The Soviets applied the Kremlin's right, under the Brezhnev doctrine, to extend help to such a regime[1] in the form of military intervention. The Communist regime was seen as a stooge of the Kremlin by the fierce Muslim mountain tribesmen of the country, whose way of life for centuries had involved perpetual warfare and tolerated no outside overlord.

After the Soviet intervention by force, it turned out that the USA did not accept it as a proper application of the "Brezhnev doctrine" to Afghanistan and provided massive help to the Mujahedin. The Soviet Chief of Staff voiced his objection to the venture, citing two British failures to conquer Afghanistan in the last century; he was clearly aware of the difficult terrain and the nature of the opponent. The Afghans inflicted only the second military defeat of the Bolsheviks and by far the most serious (the first was simply the failure of the victorious Red Army at the end of the civil war in 1920 to take Warsaw and turn Poland Communist, a quixotic adventure). The Soviet defeat undermined confidence in the regime not only among the population but also among the very leadership. In modern Russia change has often come after military defeat, such as the emancipation of serfs in 1861 after the Crimean War of 1854–6, the 1905 Russian Revolution, the Stolypin reforms after the Russian defeat in the war with Japan in 1905 and, most significant, the 1917 revolution after the defeat by the Germans in the First World War. And we know what happened after the Afghan defeat.

Soviet power had reached its maximum territorial extent in the early 1980s, holding areas in Afghanistan. The Russian instinct to expand when in trouble defeated its purpose in the most spectacular way in Russian history. Yet by no means all Russians have learned this lesson. Modern Russia has inherited the security obsession, and

---

[1] There is a curious parallel here between not letting a Communist regime become renegade to Moscow and the tsarist law which forbade reconversion to another faith (Catholic, Protestant or Muslim) for those who had already converted to the Russian Orthodox faith.

Zhirinovsky fully exemplifies it. The countries of the Near-Abroad that he wishes to occupy are to be put in quarantine by having buffer zones around them, although he would refer to these as part of Russia and does not speak of buffer zones.

He is exploiting the special fears and resentments of the Russians that have accumulated over centuries, reaching a pitch in Soviet times, when Moscow was the negative center of the Western world, feared, loathed and despised. The Russians have a curious sense of isolation in their vast land, unknown to the Scandinavians or West Europeans, who jostle against each other all the time. The Russians know that their neighbors fear them, not without good reason. Yet what the Russians really want is gratitude on the part of the countries occupied by them or drawn into their sphere of influence and, more generally, to be loved to the extent of being invited in to rule—or so Zhirinovsky and his ilk imagine.

TARTAR AND TURK

Of the major invasions that have scarred the Russians' common memory, the first that lives on is that of Tartars, under the notorious Gengiz Khan, and the Golden Horde he left behind. Russia suffered the Tartar yoke for more than two centuries after 1240. This colored Russia's relations with Turkey and Central Asia thereafter. When Zhirinovsky says, "Nothing would really happen to the world if the whole Turkish nation perished," he is expressing a Tartar-tutored Russian hostility to all things Turkic and Mongol. The Central Asians and the Azeris, as well as the Turks themselves, surround the Russians, Zhirinovsky complains, and are a menace to civilization. A new pan-Turkic alliance is feared and needs to be forestalled. The Great Game played out by Russia and Britain in the nineteenth century across Eurasia, is being reenacted, with Turkey and Iran as the latter-day foils to Russia.

The Turks are not only remnants of the Tartars in ultra-nationalist

Russian eyes; they are the successors to the destroyers of Byzantium, the Ottomans who seized Constantinople in 1453. The great destiny of being the Third Rome, center of the Orthodox faith, the Russians owe, paradoxically, to the Ottomans. But they have always feared that the Turks would one day do to them what the Ottomans accomplished with Byzantium. Fear of the Turks led Muscovy to build up a formidable army, which by the 1670s was "much the largest in Europe," claims Hellie,[2] probably an overestimate, considering French and Ottoman capacities at the time. But the Russian army was certainly a force to be reckoned with by then. "In the next decade massive Turkish thrusts [into the south of Russia] from the Black Sea were painfully checked at the price of making a wilderness of much of the Ukraine."[3] Fear of the Turks was kept alive in a series of wars that the Russians lost or only perilously won; even Peter the Great was defeated and nearly overwhelmed by them. The Tartars of Crimea, the last remnants of the Golden Horde on Russian soil, were vassals of the Ottoman sultans and a thorn in the Russian flesh, kept at bay by the vigilant Cossacks for centuries. It was not until the time of Catherine the Great that Russia took to triumphing against the Turks, occupying Crimea in 1783 and encroaching along the Black Sea coast, between the rivers Bug and Dnieper, by 1792. Despite the decline of the Ottoman empire henceforward, it remained a redoubtable power. A dispute arose over the Holy Land under Turkish rule, and over Russia's championship of oppressed Orthodox populations under the Ottomans, that led to the outbreak of the Crimean War in 1854, in which the Turks fought bravely and successfully.[4] After suffering the reverse of losing Serbia and Bulgaria to Russian arms in 1877–8, the Turks gave them a drubbing in the First World War that the Russians have not forgotten.

Logically, Iran might seem the most frightening opponent of Rus-

[2] Hellie, *Enserfment and Military Change in Muscovy*, Chicago, 1917, p. 226.
[3] Perry Anderson, *Lineages of the Absolutist State*, Verso, 1974, p. 338.
[4] Nicholas Riyasanovsky, *History of Russia*, 4th edition, OUP, 1984, p. 337.

sia today, with its fundamentalist Islamic regime. The ideology, indeed, is feared, but more in Turkic Central Asia, whither it spreads mostly from Turkey, oddly enough. Iran has never won a major war against Russia. It is Turkey that is really alarming in Russian nationalist eyes. The pan-Turkic threat of an alliance of a Turkic-speaking people, from Istanbul to Baku to Samarkand, Tashkent and Almaty (Alma Ata) in Central Asia, is what Zhirinovsky hopes to thwart with his Last Dash to the South, while, in order to round out the borders and obtain access to the Indian Ocean, Iran and Afghanistan are to be occupied as well. Zhirinovsky is determined to get in his rataliation first.

BESSARABIAN STAKES

Another nearby state with a special relationship with the Roman Empire and its own brand of Orthodox Christianity is Romania, the land of Dracula, of Vlad the Impaler, who left his enemies to die on stakes. Romanians have a Latin language and are convinced that they descend from the Roman legionaries left behind in Dacia, the Roman province there in the third century, a fact impossible to establish, since recurrent nomadic invasion has left a gaping hole in the historical record of the next millennium of Romanian history.[5] In the thirteenth century Wallachia and Moldavia, Romania's two main provinces, fell under Ottoman vassalage. Bessarabia, a strip of fertile, vine-growing territory stretching between the Pruth and the Dniester down to the Black Sea, has long been a bone of contention between the Russians and the Romanians. In modern times Russia took it in 1812 in the aftermath of expelling Napoleon. It was reunited with Romania in 1918–19 to form a Great Romanian state with Transylvania, populated by Romanians, Hungarians and Saxons.

[5] H. H. Stahl, *Les anciennes communautés villageoises roumaines, asservissement et pénétration capitalistes*, Bucharest, 1969, pp. 1–45.

In 1939 Stalin made a pact with Hitler, under one term of which the USSR could retake Bessarabia, which it duly did in June 1940. Realizing its strategic significance for the whole Black Sea area, Stalin detached the southern coastline and put it into Ukraine, while the remainder of Bessarabia, together with Trans-Dniestra, on the left bank of the Dniester, hosting a strong Soviet garrison, formed the Moldovan Soviet Republic. In 1989 this became independent Moldova. Its national identity has been troubled by three developments. One is that nationalists crave reunion with Romania; the second is that the Russians and Ukrainians of Trans-Dniestra want to rejoin Russia or Ukraine; the third is that 180,000 Turkic-speaking people, the Christian Gagauz, want secession in the south. After a war from 1989 until July 1992 between the right-bank Moldovans and Trans-Dniestra was brought to a close by the arrival of the Russian 14th Army "Peacekeepers" an uneasy truce remains.

The commander of the 14th Army, General Alexander Lebed, proud possessor of the Cossack Cross for the defense of Trans-Dniestra, is a warm supporter of Zhirinovsky. Zhirinovsky himself is right behind the Trans-Dniestra Russian cause. The Romanians, among whom he would include the Moldovans, are "Italian gypsies." Romania is an "artificial country"; it is Russians, not upstart Romanians, who are the true heirs of Rome. The Romanians are to be put in their place, losing Transylvania and roaming around a truncated Moldavia and Wallachia in Zhirinovsky's future Europe. Bessarabia and Trans-Dniestra are to return to Russia. Moldova will be wiped off the map.

This boost to Hungary, this free present of somebody else's land, is coupled by a curious detachment toward the Hungarians on the part of Zhirinovsky; as Magyars, not Slavs, they do not seem to interest him. True, on passing through Budapest in February, he nearly missed a plane and called them "the whore nation," but this is just his customary temper. There is no reason to infer any special Magyar irritation.

BULGARIAN BRETHREN

The Bulgars are Slav brothers for Zhirinovsky, fit to belong to his greater Slav union. As an Orthodox country, Bulgaria is targeted as a key state for pan-Slavism. But the Bulgarians, despite being liberated from Ottoman rule in 1878 by the Russians, are now averse to Russian domination, having endured four decades of it in the 1949–89 period, a sufficient inoculation against pan-Slavic temptations.

THE ALOOF CZECHS AND SLOVAKS

The Czechs were the least anti-Russian Catholic Slav people before 1939. But forty years of forced Communist rule, and the crushing of the Prague Spring in August 1968 (bringing to an end Dubček's Communism with a human face), make it unlikely that the Czechs and Slovaks hanker after union with Russia, when they cannot abide union even with each other. Zhirinovsky's "Fascism with a human face" is not likely to go down well in the Czech republic, whose predecessor state, Czechoslovakia, was the sole liberal democracy in Central Europe surrounded by Fascist power between the two world wars.

THE LURE AND MENACE OF GREATER GERMANY

The one foreign country that Zhirinovsky respects, and even admires, is Germany. In this he is like many of his countrymen, who remember both the great contribution Germany has made to their civilization and the devastating invasions that it has successively inflicted upon the Russians.

The Hanseatic League of trading cities, along the North Sea and the Baltic, to which Nizhny Novgorod owed its pre-eminence in the Middle Ages, brought a rich trade in timber, fur, wax, honey and wines to medieval Russia, as well as valuable cultural links with the West. But the Teutonic knights, renowned at the time for their depredations and cold, methodical brutality, pressed ever eastwards in the Middle Ages. Every Russian knows the story of how Alexander Nevski beat them on the thawing ice of Lake Peipus in April 1242, into which the knights and their mounts sank (memorably evoked by Eisenstein's film of the same name).

The Romanov tsars renewed their line by marrying German princesses, giving Russia her greatest empress, Catherine the Great (1762–96). German thought and culture pervaded the St. Petersburg court and intellectual life, Hegel having a huge influence, even more than the French, although French was the international language of aristocracy in the eighteenth century. German settlers played a valuable part in improving industry, commerce and banking at this time. Zhirinovsky is insistent that the Volga and other Germans are very welcome in Russia and could facilitate a German–Russian alliance, which he strongly favors at times.

The reason why the last qualification is necessary in the case of Zhirinovsky and many other Russians is that the twentieth century has brought the horrors of two world wars, which the Russians attribute to German mischief in 1914 and German malice in 1941, as they also do the Bolshevik Revolution of 1917. The Bolshevik takeover, the Russians believe, would have been impossible if the Germans had not allowed Lenin through in a sealed train from Switzerland to St. Petersburg in April 1917. In many Russian eyes a German Jewish thinker, Karl Marx, and his reputedly half-German follower Lenin visited this calamity upon Russia. It was defeat at the hands of Germany, first at Tannenberg in 1914 (a kind of re-enactment of the great battle of 1410 but going the other way), then more comprehensively in 1917, that gave Lenin his chance.

The Nazis were in some sense the successors of the Teutonic knights in Barbarossa (the name of the campaign), who laid waste wherever they invaded and, turning prisoners of war into slave labor, worked them to death. It cost Russia 20 million lives to oust the Germans in the "Great Patriotic War" of 1941–5. Fear of another German attack accounted mainly for Russia's occupation of Central Europe in 1945 and hence for the Cold War. No country has traumatized the Russians so profoundly as Germany, and this legacy will never be forgotten or quite forgiven. Yet the phenomenal economic success of Germany after the war won the Russians' at first reluctant but then increasingly admiring respect. Stalin himself, in his last years, expressed regret that Germany had not remained an ally of Russia, for he was prepared for a long-lasting German–Russian *rapprochement*. Many Russians today would like nothing better than just such a *rapprochement*, for which German reunification has prepared the way. Zhirinovsky expresses the ambivalence of this attitude toward Germany when he talks alternately of establishing again a "common border" and of "annihilating Germany in World War III."

One way such a border could be re-established is if Russia gave back its enclave Königsberg (Kaliningrad) in East Prussia, between Lithuania and Poland. An old Hanseatic League town, and home of Emmanuel Kant, Königsberg was seized by Stalin in 1945 and repopulated by Russians. (Either the German inhabitants fled to Germany or, of those who remained, one part died of hunger and cold while the rest were deported to Siberia.) The common border would still come about only if Lithuania and Poland were truncated, both of which possibilities Zhirinovsky has contemplated. Kaliningrad is of little use to Russia, except as a garrison.[6] However, the Russian armed forces regard it as very important in that role. It is estimated that there are 200,000 Russian troops there with very modern weapons, and troops withdrawn from the Baltic states, Poland and Germany are stationed in the area. A formidable military force

[6] It is not quite such a garrison town as Lermontov in *A Hero of Our Times*. Times have, indeed, moved on. Littered with scrap metal and the debris of an empire, Kaliningrad is a dump in the literal sense of the word.

is being built up, which causes concern not only to the Balts and the Poles but also to Germany and Sweden. Zhirinovsky's plans are, therefore, hardly likely to please the Russian military high command.

Zhirinovsky may well have concession to Germany as his trump card with which to woo the Germans to his cause. There is no doubt that repossession of Königsberg (as it would be immediately renamed) would be an offer that the Germans would find difficult to resist, genuine and heart-felt as their abdication of irredentist aspirations now is.

The two states enclosing Kaliningrad, Lithuania and Poland, played an unusually significant role in early Russian history. Russia developed its original Byzantine identity in a contest with Lithuania, a large, backward state on the Baltic only belatedly converted to Christianity, which by the late fourteenth century had an empire stretching from the Baltic to the Black Sea, including White Russia and Ukraine. The distended Lithuanian state was largely Russified in language and customs. In 1386, however, it allied itself with Poland, and after failure in 1399 against the Mongols the Lithuanians joined the Poles to win the great battle of Tannenberg in 1410. Lithuania redirected itself westwards towards Poland and came heavily under its influence long before its formal inclusion into Poland with the Union of Lublin in 1569.

Zhirinovsky considers Lithuania the one Baltic state with a right to exist, albeit in a truncated form. Although Russia occupied it in 1914, this was only by reason of its earlier incorporation into Poland, whose Lithuanian east was incorporated into Russia in 1795 in the Third Partition of Poland. Since an independent Poland should cease to exist, having been Russian in 1914, so its incorporation of Lithuania in 1569 should be annulled by tolerating an autonomous Lithuania today.

Poland has long had a complex relationship with Russia. A powerful state in the Middle Ages, Poland made a bid for the control of Russia at the "Time of Troubles" in 1603–14.

The Poles backed a pretender to the failing line of the Ruriks, the false Dimitri, who ruled for a brief period. The Poles then backed a second false Dimitri without success. After his fall the Poles declared war upon Moscow, and Russia finally rallied against the threat of occupation by heretical Catholic Poles with the new Romanov dynasty, established in 1613.

Poland remained a source of disruption in Russian eyes until it was partitioned in three stages, in 1772, 1793 and 1795. Despite Russia's subjugation of Poland, the Russians remained afraid of a Polish conquest of their Russian lands, which actually occurred in a "Time of Troubles" in 1917–20. The Red Army marched on Warsaw, but in a heroic resistance the Poles, helped by the French, repelled them. This gave them a reprieve for twenty-five years.

Poland is feared by the Russians, not just on its own account, as the intruder at times of troubles but also as occupying the historic route taken by Western invaders, latterly Napoleon and Hitler. For more reasons than one, nervous Russian nationalists have always wanted to subjugate Poland, and Zhirinovsky, at least verbally, is promising this to them.

FINLAND THE BRAVE

Finland was for centuries the easternmost province of Sweden. The army of Charles XII of Sweden was defeated by Peter the Great at Poltova in southern Ukraine in 1709. In 1808–9 Alexander I fought and defeated Sweden. Russia took over Finland, Finland becoming a Grand Duchy, with the tsar as Grand Duke. The Finns were given considerable autonomy at first, and good fighters were used by the Russians to quell periodic Polish revolts. But from the 1890s St. Petersburg followed a policy of Russification that swiftly alienated the Finns, who thenceforward gave sanctuary from the attention of the tsarist police to many Russian revolutionaries, notably Lenin and senior Bolsheviks. For several crucial months of counter-revolution in the summer of 1917 Lenin took refuge in Helsinki, from where he was able to direct preparations for the October Revolution. The revolution proved to be of benefit to the Finns, who took their chance to become independent.

Finland is now about to become a member of the European Union. Zhirinovsky's call for the Russian occupation of Finland is a rhetorical flourish and probably not much more than that. By talking of reincorporating Finland, Poland and Alaska (which was Russian between 1799 and 1867), he is reminding his listeners that his aim is to recreate the glories of tsarist Russia, not those of the Soviet Union. Even he must realize that the West would not tolerate occupation of any one of these territories, but for the moment his only concern is to maximize his appeal to Russian voters.

AREAS THAT FORMED PART OF THE OLD TSARIST EMPIRE

Zhirinovsky, like Hitler before him, is fond of cartography. He was interviewed in December 1993 by Rolf Gauffin, the former Swedish ambassador to Moscow, who was visiting the capital for the Italian geopolitical review, *Limes*. On the wall behind the LDPR's leader was his party's emblem, a stylized map of the former Russian Empire, which included Finland and Alaska. It was surmounted by an eagle and the words "Liberty and Law." "**Liberty and Law . . . and Russia,**" declared Zhirinovsky, placing his pointer on Alaska.

This interview yielded another even more interesting map, the continent of Europe as seen by Zhirinovsky. Its salient features, drawn sketchily by him with a pen, involve:

1. Poland to be divided between Germany and Russia;
2. Germany to take over Austria, the Czech republic and Slovenia;
3. Russia to take over the Baltic republics (apart from Tallinn and Kaunas);

4. Bulgaria to take over Macedonia and parts of Greece, Turkey and Romania;
5. Russia to take over Ukraine, Moldova and probably Slovakia;
6. The UN out of the former Yugoslavia;
7. The final flourish . . .

Zhirinovsky arrogantly signs his own name. This map was published in *Le Monde*, the French daily, on 29 January 1994. It was republished in color in *The European* of 3–8 February. He told Gauffin: **This Greater Germany and the new Russia will one day form an alliance that will neutralize Europe.**

Zhirinovsky said that the return to Germany of Königsberg would be **a present from Russia.** (*The European*, 3.2.94)

The map shows Poland once again divided between Russia and Germany. This would be the fifth partition of Poland. All the Poles get as compensation is Lvov, capital of western Ukraine.

The Baltic states are swallowed up by Russia. But Tallinn, capital of Estonia, escapes this fate and becomes a city-state like Liechtenstein or Luxembourg. Kaunas, former capital of Lithuania, also becomes a city-state. Germany repeats its adventures of the 1930s and obtains Austria and the Czech Republic as well as its half of Poland; meanwhile Belarus, Ukraine and Moldova become part of Russia, as does Slovakia.

As an alternative, Zhirinovsky says, Slovakia could be the nucleus of an eastern European economic community. The LDPR leader expresses his firm advocacy of Slav interests in a "greater Bulgaria," which would absorb areas of Greece, Turkey, Romania and the former Yugoslav republic of Macedonia.

Hungary would take Transylvania from Romania, which, Zhirinovosky states, **"is not a country, but only a space where Italian gypsies live."** Croatia and Serbia would divide Bosnia between them. For Zhirinovsky, **The whole of the Transcaucasus is a nest of bandits and crooks of no interest to Russia.**

Here, as in Central Asia, there will be **all-out war.** All this is highly reminiscent of the 1930s and, in particular, of the Nazi–Soviet pact of August 1939, which made certain the outbreak of the Second World War. This pact, negotiated by Foreign Minister Ribbentrop of Germany and Stalin in the Kremlin, involved the fourth partition of Poland and the confirmation of, or agreement to, territorial changes very much in the spirit of Zhirinovsky's map. The LDPR leader likes to dissociate himself from Hitler, who was, of course, the guiding spirit behind the pact on the German side. It is not hard to see why the publication of Zhirinovsky's map should have set off alarm bells once again in all of Europe's chancelleries in early 1994, nor why he has a lot to live down if he wishes to make clear to the world that he's not a "Russian Hitler" (*Le Monde*, 29.1.94, *The European*, 3.2.94).

On the famous map showing the borders of central and East European countries redrawn by Zhirinovsky, western Poland is annexed to Germany, but Poland gets back some of the territories annexed by the Soviet Union after the Second World War that now are part of Ukraine. A month or so later, during his visit to Poland, he repudiated any earlier suggestion that Poland would have to cede territory to Russia. How about Poland? **Well, Prussia used to be a German state which included Breslau (Wroclaw) and Stettin (Szczecin); these areas should be annexed to Germany. Poland can have the area around Lvov, in compensation for the loss of territory along its western frontier.** (*Die Welt*, 29.1.94).

On 8 February 1994 Zhirinovsky gave an interview on Czech television in which he confirmed that he had been invited by the Czech Republican Party, led by Miroslav Sladek, to visit the Czech Republic, a visit that was several times postponed, given the Czech government's express hostility to it. This is easy to understand in the light of his many aggressive utterances about central Europe, echoed in this very interview, in which Zhirinovsky made a verbal attack on President Vaclav Havel as well as painting a lurid picture of the Czechs' future: **If Vaclav Havel feels unhappy about my visit, then**

I am also unhappy about the fact that playwrights can become presidents of certain countries.

This is not right. I am not going to write theater plays, I am not going to write *The Cherry Orchard* if I am not Chekhov. Why, then, is a playwright a president? Your country is dying. I can assure you that in ten years' time there will be no Moravia, no Sudeten. In ten years' time the entire Czech nation will curse Havel, as the Russian people are cursing Gorbachev. All, including me, used to applaud him—after Chernenko we saw Gorbachev as a good option. Nowadays we curse that villain.

The same situation will exist in your country. Vaclav Havel will die, and in ten years' time young Czechs will curse him. They will be forced to speak German; they will be forced to forgo their mother tongue; they will be forced to attend Holy Mass in German churches and to clean the boots of German officers. This will be the Czechs' fate in a few years' time.

We do not want this. We intend to call a congress of Slavonic nations on 2 and 3 April. We are 300 million. We will live in our East European community and will not serve Western Europe. (Czech TV1, Prague, 8.2.94)

I would not like anybody to think, even theoretically, that the Polish borders should be changed, ever; we are for a strong Poland, so that Russia and Poland can be good neighbors (UPI, 12.3.94). This statement is, however, somewhat weakened by another of his announcements made at the same time: **Poland can never be a corridor for foreign armies for aggression toward Russia** (MON, 12.3.94).

Zhirinovsky was a guest of Janusz Bryczkowski, leader of the Polish right-wing National Self-defense Front. Bryczkowski announced in his opening speech of the first congress of his party that it was "ideologically associated" with Zhirinovsky. He added, moreover,

39

that the guarantor of borders in Europe was a strong Russia: "Let no one think that NATO is the guarantor of our borders."

Russia has no territorial claim and its army would never go west, stated Zhirinovsky, adding that there was a need for pan-Slavic solidarity, in which both Russia and Poland would have an immense role to play (MON, 12.3.94). Elaborating this suggestion: **If Poland and the other Slavic countries want it, Russia will be ready to establish a political alliance** (UPI, 12.3.94).

What does such a plan entail? **There would be our common army with equal rights—not a situation where Poles will be shining the shoes of German officers. They are drawing you into NATO to turn you into cannon fodder** (UPI, 12.3.94). Bryczkowsky, the Polish National Front leader, was invited to attend the World Congress of Slavonic Nations in Moscow in April.

When in Warsaw in March 1994, Zhirinovsky hobnobbed with Janusz Bryczkowsky, who not only regards Zhirinovsky as "Poland's great friend" but also sees him as Russia's future president. Bryczkowsky himself intends to run for the presidency of Poland. Zhirinovsky plans to set up a pan-Slavic union under Russian leadership, stretching from the Adriatic to the Baltic. **We have enough potential to become the most powerful community on this planet. We have the largest territory and our reserves are sufficient for Europe's development for the next three hundred years . . . I want Poles to be rich and drive Mercedes and Lincolns instead of cleaning their windows . . .** Polish soldiers should be **a part of the Slavonic army with equal rights** instead of letting themselves be dragged into a situation where they would be NATO's cannon fodder . . . (On Polish-Russian relations) **May there always be only flowers and the smiles of Polish girls, the most beautiful in the world, between us . . . The best borders are sea borders. May the Baltic Sea be the common border of Russia, Poland and Germany. In all conflicts** up to now these three countries have been the losers, while others have won. Now we want the opposite to happen. (*The Warsaw Voice*, 20.3.94)

Zhirinovsky invokes the heritage of the Soviet liberation of Czechoslovakia and Central Europe as a whole from Nazism in 1944. **Why did they enter Prague on 9 May? Why did millions shed their blood? Today they insult us there. They have erected a monument to Bandera; they have erected monuments to SS men. What about our army and the older generation? They are spat upon today. Why did they shed their blood?** (Soviet Television, 31.5.91)

The Czech Republic will one day belong to Germany . . . One day Slovakia will belong to Russia . . . Hungary wants to protect its population in Romania. (*Die Welt*, 29.1.94)

Zhirinovsky makes frequent visits to the Balkans, especially to his beloved Serbia. To do this he has to fly via Budapest. In February he burst into Budapest airport two minutes before take-off for a flight back to Moscow. The check-in for the morning flight was already closed. "I am a Member of Parliament. Hold the plane! I have to leave," he shouted in Russian. Startled officials of MALEV Hungarian Airlines, after some hesitation, requested the plane to wait. As other passengers gaped in astonishment, Zhirinovsky ordered his aides to bring forward a motley collection of baggage, cardboard boxes and what appeared to be paintings in foam wrapping. Airport security guards gathered around him nervously as he searched for his ticket, berating his assistants for incompetence. He finally found it in his own pocket. As a small mountain of luggage began to accumulate, MALEV officials balked at loading it on to the plane. "I have a first-class ticket. I want to take that luggage on the plane," Zhirinovsky shouted at a flustered check-in clerk. "If something is lost or broken, I will have your head," he warned the attendant. A MALEV official stepped forward and told Zhirinovsky that it would be impossible to load so many things on to the plane. "You'll see what is impossible when I become president," Zhirinovsky retorted. Approached by reporters, he whirled round to vent his wrath. "You have a whore-house in your country. Imbeciles!" (*Guardian*, 17.2.94)

Romania, an artificial country—did not exist before the First World War. Consequently, Dobrudja belongs to Bulgaria. The rest of the land will belong to Romania. The population there comes from Italy. (*Die Welt*, 29.1.94)

Zhirinovsky was ordered out of Bulgaria in late December 1993 after publicly urging Bulgarians to replace President Zelyu Zhelev with the Russian politician's own aide. Mr Zhirinovsky proposed the candidature of Mr. Zvetoslav Stoilov, a Bulgarian living abroad and one of Zhirinovsky's advisers, for the presidential office. He went on to say that Mr. Stoilov was an outstanding economist and his adviser on economic matters. **I'd like, and it would also be in Russia's interest, to see Mr. Stoilov, who is an outstanding economist, as Bulgarian president** (BTA News Agency, Sofia, 26.12 93). According to the LDPR leader, it is just such a president that Bulgaria needs. And the relations in the Balkans will stabilize only after he steps into office. Zhirinovsky's nominee is quite unknown in Bulgaria.

My expulsion was an act of jealousy by Zhelev. People were coming to greet me, to embrace me, to say, 'Long live Zhirinovsky, Russia's future president.' They kissed my hand, something they have never done to Zhelev. (*New York Times*, 30.12.93). Zhirinovsky's statements are unserious, according to President Zhelev. The fact that Zhirinovsky wants to make Bulgaria the sixteenth republic is self-evident. "As for this, he is a bit late: he should have brought forward this proposal ten or fifteen years ago, when the Communists were in power and shared these views," Dr. Zhelev said.

Thrace should be returned to Bulgaria by the Greeks. And Dobrudja belongs to Bulgaria; but this is actually not our problem. (*Die Welt*, 29.1.94).

We have no use for either Poland or Finland today, in answer to a question in an interview given to *Der Spiegel* (5.1.93). When the interviewer asked him, "What about tomorrow?" he did not give a direct answer but went on about the Russian people not wanting to be irritated day after day by television pictures of people on warm beaches asking for Coca-Cola when in Russia the temperature is 20 degrees centigrade below freezing.

Finland wants Karelia back. As for that, I say that if Finland wants Karelia, then Finland must come into Russia. We will not take one single step westwards–they'll all come back to Russia one day. Then he assured the Finns that he **had nothing against Finland** but at the same time warned them: **Keep away from NATO and all the other military alliances that are directed against Russia** otherwise **Russian and German troops will fight on Finnish territory.** (*Izvestiya*, 5.4.94)

The Finns: **They are afraid of me.** (*La Stampa*, 16.12.93)

MUSLIM NEIGHBORS

The majority of mankind is interested in dissecting the Muslim world. The Muslim peril has to be eliminated. The Russian Army's last march to the south would lead it to the shores of the Indian Ocean and to the Mediterranean and would mean liberation for 20 million Kurds, hundreds of thousands of Baluchis and Push-truns. (*Los Angeles Times*, 4.3.94)

Nothing would happen to the world if the entire Turkish nation perishes, although I do not wish that upon it. (*The Last Dash to the South*)

In Ankara the plans for a Greater Turkish State have long since been prepared. Pan-Turkism threatens Russia, since it has a large

Turkic-speaking Muslim population and also a Persian-speaking one; that is a good inducement for Afghanistan, Iran and Turkey to move north . . . And Russia loses everything–the "great and talented" Turkish nation is worthy of living right in the center of the world, in the scented region, on the shores of six seas; the weak and powerless Russia, however, must perish. Is that foreseen in the history of humanity? No, that is not possible. (*Die Zeit*, 14.1.94)

In the past Russia saved the world from the Ottoman Empire, which collapsed as a result of thirty wars with Russia. Without Russia perhaps the whole of Europe would have been mad Turkish . . . Millions of people have been grateful to this day. Should then Russia not be able, and not be duty-bound, to perform her last gesture: the Dash to the South? So that Russian railways may reach there: Moscow–Delhi, Moscow–Kabul, Moscow–Indian Ocean, Moscow–Teheran, Moscow–Baghdad, Moscow–Ankara, day and night, for the economy and for the development of culture? (*Die Zeit*, 14.1.94)

The Turkish "democratic" way, which made it possible for the Turks to get everything in Europe, is much worse for us. It is *kominternism*, whereas fundamentalism is nationalism (*Le Monde*, 23.12.93). Zhirinovsky does not like *kominternism* because he identifies it with internationalism, which is, as he puts it, like living in a "communal" apartment with common bathrooms and a lot of intermingling, whereas nationalism is a self-contained apartment where you are safely behind doors and you let in only such visitors as you want to see. (See also Chapter 6.)

Zhirinovsky's attitude toward Turkey is implacable; he has not one good word for it. This may be due to his resentment for having been arrested in Turkey (see Introduction to Chapter 6) and then deported in his younger days or simply to a political matter, echoing and reinforcing anti-Turkish attitudes in Russia. In his Moscow press conference after his visit to Strasbourg in early April 1994, he declared: **Turks hate all Slavs** (ITAR TASS, Moscow World Service Radio, 15.4.94).

They will all fight among themselves and we will come in when they invite us (*Guardian*, 31.1.94). That is another piece of wish-projection on the part of Zhirinovsky. His audience, his constituency, is well aware of the danger of civil war in Russia; consequently the dream image he wants to present here is the opposite: a peaceful and strong Russia that is asked to create order in the turbulent southern regions.

That will be the moment when Russian soldiers will reach the shores of the Indian Ocean. (*Guardian*, 31.1.94)

All we want is three countries: Afghanistan, Iran and Turkey. Russia can play a historic role in saving the world from the spread of Islam, from the spread of international terrorism. (*Time*, 27.12.93)

If in Afghanistan we had had the tsar's flags instead of the red flag, we would have won. (*La Stampa*, 16.12.93)

Russian troops were right to enter Afghanistan; what was wrong was that they did so under the red flag. (*Russia Express*, No. 73, 2.3.92)

Iran can take over Azerbaijan; Armenia and Georgia will belong to Turkey. These three states [Azerbaijan, Georgia and Armenia] **have never been independent.** (*Die Welt*, 29.1.94)

With Japan, Mongolia and China we have no territorial problems. (*Die Welt*, 29.1.94)

THREE

The Russian–Serbian Axis

RUSSIAN PAN-SLAVISM

If pan-Germanism was an obvious geopolitical dimension of Nazism leading to the *Anschluss* of Austria, the seizure of the Sudetenland from Czechoslovakia and Memel from Lithuania in March 1939, it might be thought that pan-Slavism is the dimension of Zhirinovsky's program that will be initially the most dangerous force should he come to power. A new union of all Slav states, or at least of those espousing the Orthodox faith, lies behind his trips to the Balkans and would justify the annexation of eastern Ukraine and Belarus.

Pan-Slavism harks on about the ancient Slavic nation but in fact is of recent origin. Like pan-Germanism, it does not seriously predate the eighteenth century as a political force of any moment. The forced Westernization of Peter the Great profoundly humiliated the Russians and provoked a nationalist backlash that took proto-pan-Slav directions. Russia's outstanding liberal thinker in the nineteenth century, Alexander Herzen, stated, "Slavophilism or Russianism, not as theory or teaching, but as the offended national feeling . . . [was] a reaction to the foreign influence that existed from the moment Peter I . . . [the Great] caused the first beard to be shaved."[1]

The Slavophiles of Herzen's time looked back nostalgically to the Moscow period of 1340–1703, which they saw through tinted spectacles. As Berdyaev says, "Interruption is a characteristic of Russian history. Contrary to the opinion of the Slavophiles, organic is the last thing it is. Russian history has been catastrophic. The Moscow period was the worst in Russian history, the most stifling, of a peculiarly Asiatic and Tatar type, and those lovers of freedom, the Slavophiles, have idealized it in terms of their own misunderstandings of it."[2]

The Napoleonic invasion prompted a wide debate concerning whether Russia was right to become a European nation after a Western fashion or to foster and develop its Slav peoples in a new brotherhood, itself a notion borrowed from the French Revolution and German Romantic ideas of nationalism.

While the Westerners took their cue from Peter the Great and, deriding Russian backwardness, stressed the need to emulate the West, the Slavophiles extolled the virtues of the Slavs, especially the eastern Slavs under Russia's rule, including the Ukrainians and White Russians. Russia was, for them, superior to the decadent materialism of the West, personified by the bourgeois menace of England and Holland.

The Slavophiles delved into Russian history, searching for organic unity, which they found in a myriad institutions and characteristics designed to enhance their self-esteem. The people, the *narod*, were organized by the *mir*, the village council, to which all land reverted on death for reallocation among the peasants. *Sobernost*, or wholeness, was its *Leitmotif*; the humility and communality of the Russian spirit, they deemed, set them apart from the West, where egoism

[1] Taras Hunczak (ed.), *Russian Imperialism from Ivan the Terrible to the Revolution*, Rutgers University Press, 1974, p. 84.
[2] N. Berdyaev, *The Russian Idea*, Greenwood Press (reprint), 1979, p. 3.

and individualism prevailed. The focus of the Slav brotherhood, for them, was the Orthodox Church, with its universal message of truth, love and internal freedom—associated with external submission to the tsar.

Constantine Aksakov gives a good description of the ideal Slavophile commune: "A commune is a union of the people who have renounced their egoism, their individuality, and wish to express their common accord; this is an act of love, a noble Christian act . . . a commune thus represents a moral choir . . . a brotherhood, a commune—a triumph of human spirit.[3]

CONTRADICTIONS OF PAN-SLAVISM

Slavophilism had arisen independently in Bohemia, Poland and the Slav lands under the yoke of Turkey, Serbia, Croatia and Slovenia. But the Polish Slavophiles regarded themselves as the natural leaders of the Slav peoples as Catholics and as Westerners despite their suffering the indignity of foreign occupation at the hand of the Russians.

The Russian Slavophiles, of course, saw themselves as the obvious leaders, the Russian empire having the vocation to incorporate all Slavs, not just the Poles in 1772–95, under its hegemony; Herzen talks of "Slavophilism or Russianism" indifferently. This is the nub of the contradiction of Slavophilism, since non-Russian Slavs are none too keen on this Russian interpretation of the matter. Pan-Slavism is a complex idea, aspiring to an impossible project, the union of highly disparate peoples, the main divide being between the Catholic Slavs of Poland, Bohemia, Slovenia and Croatia and the Orthodox ones of Russia, White Russia, Ukraine, Bulgaria and Serbia.

[3] *Russian Imperialism from Ivan the Terrible to the Revolution*, ed. Taras Hunczak, Rutgers University Press, 1974, p.86.

THE SERBIAN EXCEPTION

When Serbia and Montenegro declared war on their occupiers, the Turks, in 1876, Pan-Slavism ceased to be a vague sentiment confined to intellectuals and came alive among the general public. Pan-Slavic committees were formed and sent 5,000 volunteers, ranging from nobles to peasants and including 800 former Russian officers, to fight in the Serbian army, which was headed by another Russian volunteer, General Mikhail Cherniaev. But the Turks defeated the Serbs, as they had the Bulgarians, also in 1876.

Pressure mounted on the Russian government to intervene. Russia declared war on Turkey in 1877, obtaining victory by 1878 and the independence of Serbia and Bulgaria. It is the memory of Russian volunteers and armies then that kindled the cheers for Russian peace-keeping forces when they came to Bosnia in spring 1994.

Pan-Slavism became entrenched among educated strata of society, especially the Army, the Church and a section of the gentry, even though the tsars and the high nobility tended to disdain it, when they did not use it as a cloak for extending Russia's power, as in 1877–8. The mass of the peasantry was still largely unaffected by, if not indifferent to, other Slav peoples, whose languages and countries they knew little about.[4] Indeed, the greatest pan-Slav affair, as it was presented at the time, Russia's participation in the First World War on Serbia's side against Austria–Hungary and the German Empire up to 1917, became highly unpopular with the peasant conscript soldiers, leading to mass desertions and the revolution of 1917.

MODERN PAN-SLAVISM

Under the Soviet Union pan-Slavism was officially frowned upon, although it remained an undercurrent, giving reality to "proletarian

[4] Ibid.

internationalism" among its Slav republics and with Bulgaria. In one way the Soviet epoch gave pan-Slavism a covert boost. One achievement of the Soviet regime that can hardly be disputed is its education of the Soviet population, largely illiterate in 1917. Pan-Slavism could be comprehensible only to educated people, knowing some history of Russia, Ukraine and the former Yugoslavia and being acquainted with their religious and cultural heritage. This is by now true of many Russian citizens. Zhirinovsky has been able to benefit from this in rekindling pan-Slavism on a wider, more popular, basis. But he has implicitly redefined it as a union of Orthodox Slav peoples. Under the aegis of the LDPR Party Congress in April 1994 there was a World Congress of Slav Orthodox and Christian Nations.

Every time Zhirinovsky is acclaimed by an enthusiastic crowd in Belgrade, the TV shots back home are priceless in establishing him as the "coming man," already representing Russia's interests abroad. The Russians crave to be loved by foreigners, not pitied by them. The Serbs, in a material plight worse even than that of the Russians, manifest love and gratitude toward them in a highly gratifying way. Every Serb cheer for Zhirinovsky warms the Russians' hearts and not least Zhirinovsky himself.

There is another, and particularly poignant, link between Zhirinovsky and the Serbs. Dobrica Ćosić, a Serb nationalist intellectual, in his speech on the occasion of becoming a member of the Academy in 1977, said: "Internationalism has ruined the Serb nation." This fits in exactly with Zhirinovsky's views on the effect of internationalism on Russia, as he explained in his article published in *Izvestiya* on 28 August 1993 (see Chapter 6). Ćosić criticized the internationalism of Tito's Yugoslavia for much the same reasons as Zhirinovsky uses for condemning the Soviet "Kominternism." In addition, Ćosić, in the same speech, argued that the Serbs always win the war and lose the peace. The dire consequences of his views—no doubt shared by many other of his countrymen—are only too painfully obvious now in Bosnia.

THE ROLE OF ORTHODOXY

There are suggestions that the Greek Orthodox Church may be one determining factor in the shaping of Russian society and in the evolution (or lack of it) of its political order.

The role of the Orthodox Church at present is unclear. It certainly plays a part in efforts to reconstitute Russia as it was before the onset of the Soviet Communist regime. It is a tradition that people can go back to. However, it is difficult to say how strong religious faith is in Russian society after many decades of persecution by the Bolshevik authorities and as a result of the concomitant secularization of society.

There are those who argue that persecution saved the Orthodox faith from the kind of secularizing forces that have been eroding Western Churches during the same period by the shifting of emphasis to the political and moral aspects of religion at the expense of purely spiritual values, the core tenets of faith, the inner life, the pilgrimage of the soul through life toward God. In Protestant and, perhaps to a lesser extent, in Catholic countries of the West religion is being gradually absorbed by society and by social and political institutions. The slow erosion of dogma by detached rationalism and by science is emptying faith of its content. Christianity is reduced to its generally accepted moral values—or so goes the reasoning. Materialist pursuits undoubtedly weaken the role of faith in people's lives: the transcendental, spiritual hope of religion is replaced by short-term "realistic," "realizable" hopes of achieving material and social objectives. On the other hand, the persecution of religion may push the Church into the role of representing national objectives, that is, representing aspirations of national identity, and in the long term that may be to the detriment of the Church: when nationalist objectives have been achieved people may slowly turn away from religion. That danger threatens the Russian Church probably less than, say, the Polish Catholic Church or, more significantly, the Serbian Orthodox

Church, which is at present closely identified with the Serbian cause of expansion.

The idea of Orthodox brotherhood plays an important part in bolstering Russian support for the Serbs. That is certainly exploited by Zhirinovsky, as the religious factor in the Balkan conflict is thought to become more important. There is another aspect of Orthodoxy that has influenced Russian history throughout the centuries. As a result of the fall of Constantinople to the Ottomans, the role of Byzantium as the champion of the Christian faith against the infidel fell vacant. Ivan III, by marrying the niece of the last Byzantine emperor, assumed that role and declared Moscow the successor of Byzantium: the Third Rome. The messianic spirit resulting from this new legitimacy of Moscow has been kept alive ever since in one form or another. It can be argued that Communism, shedding any Christian aspect, continued this mission by trying to construct a terrestrial paradise, justifying expansionism and moral superiority on the basis of it. Berdyaev maintains that "Messianic consciousness is more characteristic of the Russians than of any other people except the Jews."[5]

What are those aspects of the Orthodox faith that may also have influenced Russian society in its adherence to autocratic rule and have facilitated its acceptance by the population? It is remarkable that in Orthodox iconography the image of Christ the King (Pantocrator) has always been much more prevalent than in Western Christianity. A second point is that the Orthodox Church has never accepted the idea of Purgatory, which was devised in Western Christianity in the Middle Ages to play a mediating role between damnation and salvation. The propensity for extremes has always been held to be an important feature of the "Russian character."

[5] N. Berdyaev, *The Russian Idea*, Greenwood press (reprint), Westport, 1979, p.8.

ZHIRINOVSKY MAKES HIS FIRST TRIP TO SERBIA

At a press conference in Belgrade's Yugoslavia Hotel on 30 January 1994 Zhirinovsky warned Western politicians that **bombing Serb positions in Bosnia would be a declaration of war against Russia.** (Tanjug, Belgrade, 30.1.94).

Speaking in detail about the ways to solve the conflict in Bosnia-Hercegovina, he said that there were three ways to end it: the foreign troops should leave the territory of former Yugoslavia and let the Slav nations solve their problems on their own; **the status quo should be accepted; or Russian troops should be allowed in.** The latter course is exactly what happened in late February—yet another instance of Russian foreign policy, this time with Western approval, taking a leaf out of Zhirinovsky's book.

We are supporting the Serbs and our standpoint is that the Serb lands—the Serbian republic [in Bosnia-Hercegovina] **and the Republic of Serbian Krajina—should be within the Republic of Serbia,** he said, adding that he would be happy if **Russia and Serbia had a common border** (Tanjug, Belgrade, 30.1.94)

On 30 January 1994 Zhirinovsky arrived in Subotica from Slovenia, on his way to Belgrade. He had been invited to Serbia by the Serbian Democratic Party of the Serbian Lands (the leading party in the Serbian Republic in Bosnia-Hercegovina). After a brief traditional Orthodox ceremony Zhirinovsky addressed Subotica's citizens. **I am coming to your country for the first time, but I am coming here as a representative of the victorious party at the Russian elections, as a representative of Russia, which has chosen a new course. This course is the obligation of Russia to help the brotherly Serbian people. Our enemies are our common enemies, and you ought to know that they will be punished for all the evils committed against the Slav people** (Montenegrin TV, Podgorica, 30.1.94).

A new era is beginning, Zhirinovsky said. His words were accompanied by chanting: "Russia! Serbia!" He stressed that the enemies of the Slav people were now trembling in Paris, Bonn, London, Washington and Tel Aviv.

Commenting on the war the Serbian people were waging on the territory of the former Yugoslavia, Zhirinovsky said that **all the barbarians who had settled on the sacred Serbian soil had to accept the fact that this land belonged to the Serbian people or leave it** (Hungarian Radio, Budapest, 30.1.94).

THE WEST IS BLAMED FOR WAR IN FORMER YUGOSLAVIA

On 31 January 1994 in Vukovar, in the Republic of Serbian Krajina, Zhirinovsky said that **the West—because of applying double standards–was most to blame for the war in the former Yugoslavia.** On the one hand, the republics that seceded from the former Yugoslavia were recognized and, on the other hand, the Serbs were not granted the right to self-determination.

The West must be punished for this, and Russia will do its utmost to have war criminals punished, Zhirinovsky said at a press conference held in the partially rebuilt Danube Hotel after the rally. Amidst an ovation from several thousand people in Vukovar, the guest of the Serbian Democratic Party of the Serbian Lands promised that **the great Russia will be the protector of all Serbs** and spoke about the **creation of a joint Slav state from Vladivostok to Knin.** (Tanjug, Belgrade, 31.1.94).

SOLIDARITY WITH ZHIRINOVSKY'S "SERBIAN BRETHREN"

On 1 February, in Podgorica, Zhirinovsky told a meeting of several tens of thousands of its residents that there were 300,000 Russian soldiers in Germany. **If the Germans have lost their appetite for war, if necessary we will transfer those 300,000 soldiers from Germany into the Balkans and help the Serbs** (Tanjug, Belgrade,

1.2.94), he said to a standing ovation and frequent shouts of "Russia! Russia!" and "Vladimir! Vladimir!" **The world should be told what Russian military might is. We have state-of-the-art weaponry, which others do not have,** the leader of the Russian liberals said, recalling the battles won by the Russians in past eras and during this century.

Zhirinovsky stressed that **again Russia had a great historic mission, that of preventing the Slav peoples from being converted to Catholicism or Islam. Let the Catholics stay in Paris and Madrid,** he said. **Russians and Serbs have two enemies now—Catholicism and Muslims. Religion is used as the final weapon,** Zhirinovsky stressed.

Addressing his audience mainly as **brother Serbs,** although he occasionally mentioned Montenegrins, Zhirinovsky also announced that he would convene an assembly of the political parties of Slav states in early April 1994 in Moscow to proclaim the idea of forming an East European community.

We are one nation; we have one religion. If they have formed a European Union in the West, we will form an East European community. Territorially, it will be ten times larger than the European Union. We are spiritually stronger than the West. We have the greatest economic potential.

He stressed clearly in Podgorica that any possible bombing of the Serbs in Bosnia would mean a declaration of war on Russia and that in the post-war period the Serbs in the Balkans would get **everything they need** from Russia. With the victory of his party, Zhirinovsky said, **The Russian people had determined a new course in policy, particularly toward the events in the former Yugoslavia . . . The world wants to divide the Balkans into many little statelets, so that the West can Catholicize half the peninsula and Islamize the other half. They are trying to destroy our Orthodox religion, and your only fault is that you are on the borders with the West, and therefore the attacks on you are all the fiercer.**

As for the sanctions, they can keep them in force. Russia has all you need and will buy everything you can offer. As for defense, if there is an attack, you should not give it so much as a thought.

Russia has not only state-of-the-art weapons, but also a secret sonar weapon—as it is called—which it will use for its own defense and for the defense of its Orthodox brothers on the territory of the former Yugoslavia. (For more on his "secret weapon" see Chapter 5.) **Russian might has to be displayed to the world so as to force it to leave the Slavs to live in peace. Russia will make it clear that Serbia should not be taken lightly.**

At the end of his speech, Zhirinovsky called on Russians and Serbs to **become closer in all aspects. Russians, who will pay for everything, should have holidays on Adriatic beaches.** (Tanjug, Belgrade, 1.2 94; Serbian Radio, Belgrade, 1.2.94).

AIR STRIKE ON SERBS WILL BE THE "BEGINNING OF THE THIRD WORLD WAR"

In an interview with Czech TV on 8 February 1994 Zhirinovsky replied to a question about his views on the possibility of an air strike against the Serbian troops shelling Sarajevo. He said, **We oppose violence. To bomb Serbian towns is the same as bombing Russian towns. If this terrible thing takes place, we will lodge our protest with the countries whose pilots are involved in the bombing. The same thing will consequently happen to their towns—bombs will fall on towns of the countries that attack Bosnia** (Czech TV, 8.2.94).

In an address to the State Duma on 9 February Zhirinovsky said that bombing of the Serb positions in Bosnia would be the **beginning of the Third World War.** Zhirinovsky's address was connected with his recent tour of former Yugoslavia. According to him, **millions of Serbs are appealing to Russia for protection.** After a brief outline of the country's history Zhirinovsky said the people living there were **a single Orthodox people, some of whom were only forcibly converted into Islam and Catholicism.** Vladimir Zhirinovsky called on the Duma to take a unanimous position on the matter and threatened that **the countries whose pilots dare to bomb the Serb positions will be completely eliminated** (ITAR–TASS, Moscow, 9.2.94).

PLANS FOR GREATER SERBIA AND THE ALLIANCE OF SLAV PEOPLES

Srdjan Djurić, the editor of the *Eye of the World* program of the Independent Television Studio B, Belgrade, had an "exclusive" interview with Zhirinovsky, the text of which was published in the Belgrade-based journal *Večernje Novosti* on 28 January 1994. In it Zhirinovsky said: **All armies, including that of NATO, should be withdrawn from the territory of the former Yugoslavia. The existing situation needs to be strengthened, and the Yugoslav peoples themselves need to decide their future. Territories populated by Serbs or Croats must stay under the control of Serbs or Croats, while the Muslim issue is an artificial one. You do not have any Muslims.**

The blockade must be lifted and then everything will take a normal course. There will be Slovenia, Croatia and Greater Serbia, and that is it. Bosnia-Hercegovina, Montenegro—it is all Serbia. Nothing else will be necessary. Let there be three states: Slovenia as one entity and Croatia—if they are such great Catholics—and the rest will be Greater Serbia, whose borders will be shared with Bulgaria, Romania and Hungary. You have access to the Adriatic; it is all normal.

Djurić then said: "Your idea of a confederacy of Orthodox countries has been given a lot of publicity in Serbia. How do you envisage this? Which countries would it comprise? What would be its purpose?" Zhirinovsky replied: **We need to think about the fact that in this world, which has fallen apart, there are no longer two blocs; there is no bilateral balance, and no fanatical ideology lasts forever. All this has gone down the drain. Essentially, this was violence. However, if we were to try uniting into some kind of alliance of states, as Orthodox Slavs, this would make us stronger, give us a** common language with you. We are one tribe. You remained in the Balkans, the Poles proceeded to the northwest, the Russians to the northeast; our civilization started there. The Russians went on their way, the Poles on theirs and you stayed here. Then they hacked Yugoslavia to pieces, gave some to the Italians, Austrians, Germans and Turks. They are all barbarians. They came from here 500 years ago; they conquered the Byzantine Empire and kept you in blood and torture for 500 years until Alexander II liberated all of you.

That is why we could now form a Slav alliance of Slav states. The Balkans, [the] Czech [Republic], Slovakia, Poland, Russia—these would make a very good foundation because we share a common language and culture. The Serbs, the Ukrainians and the Russians are all Orthodox. It would be easier for all of us. It would all be one expanse of territory because this is a single territory, one territory, a huge territory. If you were in New Zealand and someone else were in Argentina, how could you unite? Whereas in this case everyone is here. You. The Bulgarians. Only the Hungarians and the Romanians are in the way . . . There is a clear border with the Ukraine, Belarus and Russia.

We could save a lot on transport—for example, from your ports on the Adriatic across all of Russia from Vud to Japan. There you are. Poland and Germany as well. Hamburg, Warsaw, Moscow, Vladivostok: a Eurasian transit trade route, and everything will be fine. The language—Russian. You will be pleased to speak Russian more often than English. You even use the same alphabet as we do. We favor doing something. We are trying to accomplish something. However, the Slavs have always been weak. The Germans constrained you from the west, the northeast and the northwest. If a new Russia emerges, we will not allow them to go on constraining you. If you desire closer relations with Russia, so be it. If you do not, you are welcome—everything depends on you, on your wishes. If the Russians rule over the territory of the former Soviet Union, the situation in Serbia and former Yugoslavia will be stable. If the Serbs are at war—with Croatia and Bosnia—it will be an endless war. The same applies in our case. If you remove the Russian front, we too will have an endless war, just like Afghanistan. (*Večernje Novosti*, Belgrade, 28.1.94)

ON SERBIAN AND "YUGOSLAV" LEADERS

In his interview with the Belgrade-based Independent Television Studio B's editor, Srdjan Djurić, Zhirinovsky was asked his opinion of the presidents of Serbia and former Yugoslavia. Zhirinovsky said, I do not know them very well personally. From the point of view of principles, they're all former Communists. I am not a Communist, and that is why it is obvious that there is no agreement on ideology. I am ready to support them if they take up a patriotic position—that is, where there are Serbs, that is Serbia. Zhirinovsky then asked Djurić the name of the current president of Yugoslavia, since Milošević is the president of Serbia only. Djurić replied: "His name is Lilić." Zhirinovsky then continued: Who? Lilić? Who is he? We know of Milošević from Serbia, and the Muslims have Izetbegović. Who is this Izetbegović? What makes him a Muslim? And I know Tudjman, the Croat. There, we have heard of them— Tudjman, Milošević, Izetbegović—while the president of the united Serbia and Montenegro is not widely known . . . We knew of Tito, Josip Broz Tito! That was all we knew—Tito—and nothing else. Nowadays you elect them and change them every year. For example, that American—where did he run off to? Djurić replied: "You mean Panić [a Yugoslav American who stood unsuccessfully against Milošević in the last elections for the Serbian presidency]?" Zhirinovsky said: Yes, Panić. That was his fate. He came for a while, he was here, and then he went back to where the greasy sandwiches are (*Večernje Novosti*, Belgrade, 28.1.94).

The second stage of his visit to former Yugoslavia at the end of January was Serbia. He arrived from Slovenia, via Hungary, at the town of Subotica, just south of the Hungarian–Serbian border. Subotica was, until recently, a town with an ethnic Hungarian majority.

In his speech he explained that it was the duty of Russia to help the brotherly Serbian people. As he put it: **Our enemies are our common enemies and you ought to know that they will be punished for all the evils committed against the Slav people.** And he stressed that the enemies of the Slav people were now trembling in Paris, Bonn, London and Washington (according to Hungarian Radio, he also added Tel Aviv to the list of towns). Commenting on the war in which the Serbs were involved, he said that all the barbarians who had settled on sacred Serbian soil had to accept the fact that this land belonged to the Serbian people or leave it (Montenegrin TV, 30.1.94). Later that day, in Belgrade, he focused on more immediate issues.

Bombing Serb positions in Bosnia would be a declaration of war against Russia.

The Russian Army is still in Europe—it is not threatening anyone.

We are supporting the Serbs, and our standpoint is that the Serb lands, i.e. the Serbian Republic in Bosnia-Hercegovina and the Republic of Serbian Krajina, should be within the Republic of Serbia. He added that he would be happy if **"Russia and Serbia had a common border."** (Press conference, Belgrade, 30.1.94)

I promise you that I will very soon make radical changes in policy. I have already demanded that [Foreign] **Minister Kozyrev should say clearly to the entire world that the Russian government and the Russian parliament are on the side of the Serb people.** (Zhirinovsky's speech in Bijeljina, as reported by Tanjug, Belgrade, 31.1.94). A few days later Kozyrev did indeed change his attitude more or less along the lines Zhirinovsky suggested in response to NATO's threat of air strikes.

Catholics from the West, Muslims from the East, enemies from the North—they all want to take a chunk of Greater Serbia for themselves and they think that we will agree to it. We will never agree to it, and Russia will help you. It will punish those who wish to divide the Serb land.

This policy has been going on for a hundred years now. Every fifty years they start a war in the Balkans or somewhere else, and each time the victims are the Serb and the Russian peoples. Our message to the whole world today is that a new historic era is in the making. Once and for all, we shall put an end to the policy of playing games with the destinies of the Serb and Russian peoples (Zhirinovsky's speech in Bijeljina, as reported by Tanjug, Belgrade, 31.1.94). This is a good example of Zhirinovsky's skills in demagoguery. He identifies with the Serb sense of being a beleaguered nation, constantly under attack from all sides, the self-pity of the aggressor.

His success in Serbia did not seem to be marred by the fact that his relations with the Serb leader, Milošević, are not particularly cordial. In Slovenia he announced, **He must go**, describing him as an incorrigible Communist. Both politicians are populists, but Zhirinovsky is the real thing. He is willing to incur the wrath of politicians with pronouncements like: **I have no wish to be of service to any politician.** He points out that he always has the little man in mind. That is one way in which Zhirinovsky distances himself from the entire former political élite, who spoke about the people *ad nauseam* but certainly did not want to hear what they had to say. (We remember the famous slogan of the demonstrators in the then East German city of Leipzig in autumn 1989 who shouted: "We are the people"— the people the leadership has always been talking about and through whom it had tried to justify its actions, saying, "The people want, or will not tolerate . . .") The memory of that is, of course, still very much alive in Russia, so that Zhirinovsky has to do more than simply talk about the people: he must publicly dissociate himself from other politicians, especially from the Communists, to have any kind of credibility. He takes this line also with the present "democratic" Russian leadership, accusing them of having been Communists, which indeed is true of most of them.

No doubt Milošević was comforted by Zhirinovsky's dreams of a Slavic empire stretching **from the Adriatic to Vladivostok** and the promise that Serb territory will be extended—presumably by Zhirinovsky if he becomes president of Russia—to include all lands **wherever its citizens live.** (The word "citizen" is clearly used loosely, since ethnic Serbs living in Bosnia and Croatia, etc., are not Serb but Yugoslav citizens.)

All foreign troops must leave [the former Yugoslavia]. **And the Serbs, Croatians and Bosnians should keep their present borders. The UN troops must withdraw so that the fighting factions are able to settle the conflict between themselves.** (*Die Welt*, 29.1.94)

ZHIRINOVSKY'S SPEECH TO SERBS IN CROATIA

Obviously showing signs of a drinking session or two, Zhirinovsky addressed two thousand of his fellow **brothers by blood and faith** who had been waiting for him for hours in the Croatian city of Vukovar on 2 February 1994.

Who dares say it? Who dares claim falsely that Serbia is a small country? It's not small! It's not small! Three times it has waged war! Here is an old country that has an emperor in heaven! Serbia, our dear mother, gave birth to us all. Long live Serbia!

We Slavs cannot continue to be the victims of the struggle to save Western civilization from the barbarians. The time has come to repay us for all our sacrifices. There are 300 million of us together.

I assure the governments of some Western countries that using force will not help them. If a single bomb falls on the towns of Bosnia, I warn that this means a declaration of war on Russia, and we will punish them for it. My name, Vladimir, means "ruler of the world." Let us Slavs rule the world in the twentieth century. (*Daily Mail*, 2.2.94)

The bombing of Serb positions round Gorazde inflamed Zhirinovsky's wrath toward NATO amd the West in general. **NATO's action is against Russia. For the most part, it serves the interests of Germany in the Balkans. It is against Christians, against the Slav people,** Zhirinovsky said, adding: **If I were president, we would bomb those bases in Italy. They bomb one town; we bomb another town.** (MON 11.4.94).

The official Russian reaction was not as wild, but Sergei Sakhrai, Russian Deputy Prime Minister, told reporters in the lower house of the Duma: "I think the bombing was targeted not so much at Serb positions . . . as at the internal political position in Russia . . . The national-patriots benefited from this . . . It is a blow to reforms in Russia." Such statements, in their curiously illogical way, look as if the Russian official position and Zhirinovsky were drawing closer together.

FOUR

The Far-Abroad

ATTITUDES AND PLATITUDES

Under Western Eyes

One thing that is preventing the gravity of the situation that is developing in Russia from being realized fully in the West is a range of concepts, distilled here but quite inappropriate in a Russian context. The Russians have always been very different from other Europeans; and seventy years of Communism have made them even more so. The unprecedented crisis that they are now enduring is not, despite the new trappings of liberal democracy, making them like the West at all. It is, rather, bringing out their more farouche qualities in darkened hues. At the use of *chiaroscuro* Zhirinovsky is an adept.

Westerners talk of moderates and extremists. In the West someone like Zhirinovsky inhabits the "lunatic fringe." Westerners are not aware quite how extreme the unfolding situation in Russia is, where what would be an extremist position to Westerners is a commonly held outlook. In the extremist situation, the extremist is king.

Westerners also attribute the success of extremist politics to the "protest vote." The notion of the protest vote is readily applicable to a crisis in the West. In the early 1930s, for example, Germany, having lost a world war, was engulfed in a chronic economic crisis. A humiliated nation, with 40 percent of its people out of work and a fragile democracy, gave rise to a protest vote for Hitler, one third of the electorate casting their lot for Nazi totalitarianism in 1932. This situation was not in the same league as Russia's position today. The Russian crisis is very much graver. Germany in 1933 was a country with the most advanced economy in Europe, whose woes were easily remedied by state spending on *Autobahns* and armaments. By 1936 unemployment was down to 2 percent, and the economy was booming. Russia's agony is that its present economic plight is the outcome of seven decades of intensive misdevelopment.

Nobody really knows how to rescue a broken-down, misdeveloped economy. Many pretend to, not least the IMF and the reformists. But IMF shock therapy has not succeeded in stabilizing the financial economy of Russia, while it has certainly succeeded in destabilizing its real economy. The leaders in Moscow are trying one desperate expedient after another to rectify the situation, without effect.

In this crisis everyone becomes a protest voter, the pro-reformers trying to turn Russia into a capitalist country in a hurry and protesting against the Communist heritage, the Communists protesting the loss of the Soviet empire and the Soviet Union itself, and the ultra-nationalists protesting against the degradation of the nation. When every voter is a protest voter, the likes of Zhirinovsky do well. For in Russia what is there not to protest about? An economy in ruins, a society breaking down for lack of public morality and falling into the clutches of the mafias, an environment polluted and partially radioactive, a health service in disarray, a rise in epidemics and the death rate decimating the population, the best scientists and engineers leaving the country and only the mafias functioning successfully in fleecing the country of its resources and salting away their ill-gotten gains abroad. The country is going to the dogs, and everybody knows it. This type of crisis, so much more profound and desperate than Germany's in the 1930s, breeds the politics of despair and the geopolitics of fury. Hence Zhirinovsky's outbursts, contrary to all that is politically correct in the West, are heard with glee by many sections of the population.

Under Eastern Eyes

When Zhirinovsky goes to Strasbourg, as he did in early April 1994, and chucks plants from the Russian Consulate at Jewish demonstrators, he is giving them what they deserve, according to many Russians, who blame the Jews for the Bolshevik Revolution and Communism, that thought-child of Karl Marx and Leon Trotsky. The more aggressive Zhirinovsky's utterances against the West, the more he rises in the esteem of ultra-nationalists.

Displaying contempt for the West serves the purpose of distinguishing and distancing Zhirinovsky from the present leaders of Russia as well as from what we must now call the previous generation of reformers: Gorbachev and his *entourage*. What the Russians see as the failure of the West to help Russian reforms promotes an anti-Western attitude that has been there latently at least from the time of Peter the Great and his forced modernization (i.e. Westernization).

There is, however, another source of anti-Western attitudes, the influence of early Romanticism in German eighteenth-century thought. This exerted influence on intellectuals in the first place and then percolated down society. Soviet anti-capitalism and anti-imperialism tried to make use of that latent propensity, with some success at first, but later it was much weakened by the ever more apparent failure of Communism to overtake capitalism. One of the most important points of the anti-Western movement in nineteenth-century Russia was the argument that Westerners were winning the competition in the economic and political sphere but in the process were losing their soul. The concept of the "Russian soul" is still important in present-day Russian consciousness; it is reinforced now that Russians can travel more easily to the West and see what they regard as inauthentic in the Western character: artificial, "plastic" personalities, without the existential depth of Russians. That feature was noticed in the nineteenth century by, among others, Dostoyevsky and was linked with a German early Romantic perception of the French in particular by J. G. Hamann. As a matter of fact, it was the French themselves who noticed it even earlier. À mesure que la société se perfectionne, l'homme se dégrade (To the extent that society perfects itself, man degenerates).

In the later Brezhnev years many Russians, having lost faith in the capacity of Communism to overtake the Western countries, turned into "occidentophiles." The wheel had turned to sympathy toward the West, and that transformation engulfed Soviet leadership as well— Gorbachev was clearly one who wanted to learn as much as he could from the West and to apply the medicine to Soviet society and economics. He did not realize, however, that you cannot take the best features of a capitalist society and those of Communism and work out a Third Way. The Third Way was much talked about in the Communist countries of Central and Eastern Europe around 1989 but has since been abandoned by most politicians as a hopeless quest. Zhirinovsky, however, still seems to hang on to that idea when he advocates not destroying the good features of the command economy and at the same time promoting a free-market economy (see Chapter 5).

In the 1980s many Russians were listening to Russian-language broadcasts from the West and learned something about Western society. In both Western publications and broadcasts there was criticism of the evil effects of the Soviet-style command economy and of the lack of freedom in economic life as well as in the development of society. The advantages of the free market and democracy were extolled; little mention was made, however, of the difficulty of the transition from Communism to capitalism. That gave the wrong impression to untutored listeners, who imagined that once the Soviet system was abolished everything would be fine and the West would help Russia. When, following the changes in 1991, the West dragged its feet and the expected help was not forthcoming, of course a new disillusionment with the West set in, and that is still growing. Zhirinovsky makes good use of it, and that is one of the reasons why he does not mind disparaging remarks about him in the Western media. In a television program broadcast by BBC 1 (*Panorama*, 28.1.94) he said explicitly to the British journalist interviewing him: **Go on calling me fascist and compare me with Hitler. The more you do it, the more votes I'm going to get in the next election.**

THE WEST AND FOREIGN COUNTRIES IN GENERAL

The twenty-first century will be **our century,** he predicts. **We are washing away these scabs, this dirt that has accumulated over the whole twentieth century. Sometimes this causes blood. This is bad.** But blood, he adds in a final gruesome flourish, **may be necessary in order finally to wash away this contagion that was introduced into the center of Russia from the West to poison the country and undermine it from within—through Communism, nationalism, cosmopolitanism, through the influence of alien religions, alien ideas, an alien way of life. We will put an end to this** (*The New Republic*, 14.2.94).

If the European, Asian and American great powers refuse to acquiesce in Zhirinovsky's last dash to the south, Zhirinovsky has pledged **to make life very unpleasant** (*National Review*, 21.3.94). He has never specified what his measures might be, but nuclear blackmail and the abrogation of arms-control agreements are among those measures that he has mentioned.

I feel neither particular sympathy nor particular antipathy toward any foreign statesmen. (*Der Speigel*, 51, 1993)

We must divide the spheres of influence. It is like two girls and two blokes. The men have to decide which girl is theirs and then

there are two couples, everything is friendly. Until they decide what belongs to whom, they will fight. (*The Times*, 21.12.93)

On relations with the West, Zhirinovsky said that any Western country could help Russia, but Russia did not need aid. **Russia is a country with abundant resources, and it is prepared to develop equable economic relations with all states. I understand Western businessmen who have misgivings in view of the economic situation in Russia.** (ITAR–TASS, 22.12.93)

At a press conference in Karinthia (Austria) Zhirinovsky warned the West against interfering in Russian affairs. **If certain Western circles were to provoke a civil war in Russia, nuclear and chemical weapons might get out of control . . . Russia has far more dangerous weapons than nuclear weapons . . . these weapons are "Elipton" weapons, with which the entire world could be destroyed.** (Oesterreich One Radio, 22.12.93)

We must ask ourselves, with whom are we interested in good relations? What does the West do for us? Westerners come here to buy cheap resources, to conquer our markets, to pay us slave wages. The West takes everything from us: the material products of Russia and the brains of our people. That's enough of that. (*The Times*, 21.12.93)

He aims to reverse **Gorbachev's and Yeltsin's policies of giving everything to the West** (*Financial Times*, 9.12.93). Generally speaking, he rides on the rising tide of disillusionment about the West in Russia. That is partly due to the tacit suggestion on the part of the West that once Communism and a command economy is eliminated, prosperity will emerge and the Russians will be received into the community of the well-to-do élite of the world. It is a view that has never been expressed in so many words, but people in Russia and other Communist states could not possibly have comprehended the difficulty of the transition, and before the collapse of Communism Western broadcasts rarely mentioned the size of the task. Hope was stressed at the expense of sweat and tears. Also listeners in Communist countries were assured of Western help by implication rather than by detailed explication. Similar suggestions by implication were given, for instance, to the Bosnians and the Croats at the beginning of the disintegration of Yugoslavia. Many Western countries were very reluctant to recognize the independence of former Yugoslavia's successor states. It was that very reluctance (based on practical political considerations) that awakened hopes in Croatia and Bosnia, since it clearly seemed to say: "We are unwilling to rush into it because if we do recognize their independence, then we will bear some responsibility for promoting or defending it," a fatally naïve misinterpretation.

Why should we care about what Britain or France thinks about us? Sort out your problems. Keep away from us. (*The Times*, 21.12.93)

Today our main weapons are made up of the fleet and the army. This is real power! The best borders are sea borders. England was a sea power with the best sea borders! Mongolia has no sea borders: it is a shabby state! Today we have no colonies. The colonies provided England with the lion's share of its profits. Today we receive nothing from colonies and yet feed beggarly appendages. We should be thinking about colonies. . . . I will struggle for Britain's disintegration. Let there be separate Irish, Scottish and Welsh peoples. They've suffered enough under imperial England. (*Independent* Magazine, 2.4.94)

At a press conference in Moscow after his visit as member of a Russian delegation to Strasbourg, Zhirinovsky lashed out against the West and said that if Russia joined the Council of Europe, **a struggle**

will be waged against us for your money. He also took an anti-NATO stance, saying: **We are glad that the country's political leadership has taken a correct step in that direction** (non-cooperation with NATO). **We support the president's decision not to sign the Partnership for Peace program** (ITAR–TASS, Moscow, World Service, 15.4.94). President Yeltsin did not, in fact, refuse to sign it but simply put it off until a later date, which, of course, may result in Russia's not signing it. Zhirinovsky has always been adamant that Russia should not join any Western organization because he regards such a step as limiting Russia's freedom of movement and leading to further damage inflicted on Russia by the West.

Though it no longer has an opponent [the Warsaw Pact], **NATO is drawing close to Russia's borders. It wants to send its troops to the Baltic countries and Transcaucasia, the Black Sea, the Barents Sea and the Balkans.** (*Warsaw Voice*, 20.3.94)

His visit to Strasbourg incensed him against the West in general. His heaping insults on Jewish demonstrators and throwing flower pots at them made a bad impression, something that he would normally shrug off or even welcome, but this time he may have felt that he had gone too far. However, at the Moscow press conference he vented his anger against the West, fulminating against **the Zionists and Americans.** Britain also came in for criticism. The British, he declared, **plundered the world first of all, yet now have become conservative, protecting their plunder, and have foisted their language on the whole world.** (*Warsaw Voice*, 20.3.94)

You send us the clothes you do not want to wear and the food you do not want to eat (*The Times*, 21.12.93). The anti-Western stance expressed in these statements is due as much to the topic of the day as to trying to bolster the self-respect of a population that knows itself to be at the center of an empire, however tottering, and is now completely disorientated by changes that baffle it, as they baffle its leaders. The "food you do not want to eat" probably refers to the meat sent by Britain some months earlier as food aid and found by the authorities to be unfit to eat.

I am an internationalist twice over—both as far as my primary education is concerned and as far as my secondary education is concerned. I can speak to the president of France *tête-à-tête* in his mother tongue. When we are told that our leaders have *tête-à-tête* meetings, it is untrue—interpreters are by their side. But, as for me, I will speak to him *tête-à-tête*—and with Kohl in German and with Bush in English. I have already had *tête-à-tête* conversations with them in Bonn. I removed the members of my delegation, asked the diplomats of the German Foreign Ministry to leave, and I had a *tête-à-tête* chat with Herr Schaefer, the deputy foreign minister of the Federal Republic of Germany, and Herr Genscher, the German Foreign Minister. So, I am not just theorizing now; I have already done it . . . In foreign policy we must move from a West–East relationship to a North–South relationship. It is a safer and cheaper one, giving us friends who possess a high degree of culture and technology: North America, northern Europe and Japan. Our friends today are not, unfortunately, remarkable for their culture or their riches. It is as though we have opted on purpose for the poorest, the weakest, and, in the final analysis, we ourselves have become like them. As the Russian proverb puts it: you become like those with whom you keep company. (Soviet Television, 22.5.91)

We have no use for those American false images that are thrust upon my people on television day by day . . . We do not want Pepsi-Cola at all, or chewing-gum. (*Der Spiegel*, 51, 1993)

On arriving in Helsinki to take part in a parliamentary seminar on the prospects for Russian membership of the Council of Europe, Zhirinovsky said: **We do not need your Council of Europe; we do** not ask for it. On the contrary, it is you who need us. (ITAR-TASS, Moscow, World Service English broadcast, 4.4.94)

If I accept the invitation of that politician [a conservative South African politician], it does not mean that I have anything against Negroes . . . My heartfelt desire is that the last Russian soldiers should soon leave Germany; but the American soldiers should also leave. There should be no foreign military base in Germany. Germany must have freedom without any limitations. (*Der Spiegel*, 51,1993)

I greet Paris as the town of Arabs. In ten, twenty years things will be all over for France . . . The same goes for Germany: the Turks will be in charge there. Only Russia remains a white country, the country of natural democracy, where there are human rights for all, without discrimination. (French TV Antenne 2, Paris, 10.4.94). This was said during Zhirinovsky's visit to the Council of Europe in Strasbourg as a member of the delegation of the Russian Parliament. He was not allowed to go anywhere else in France, which upset him.

The new Russian state, he says, will help France rid itself of **American and Zionist influence.** (*The New Republic*, 14.2.94)

Ethnic Germans should not leave Russia in future; on the contrary, German farmers could come and find fortune with us (*Der Spiegel*, 51,1993)

Austria and Slovenia should be one country. Germany, Austria and Slovenia should have access to the Adriatic. That is the wish of the German people. (*Die Welt*, 29.1.94)

Thrace should be returned to Bulgaria by the Greeks. And Dobrudja belongs to Bulgaria; but this is not actually our problem. (*Die Welt*, 29.1.94)

THE USA

I am against Zionists, Americans and American influence . . . American Jews make America strong, but Russian Jews make Russia weak. They do that on purpose so that they can emigrate to Israel. They should stay here . . . Our greatest problem are the Americans and the Zionists. When I come to power I'll put things in order and throw out the Americans and the mafia. (*Die Zeit*, 4.3.94)

We should maintain ordinary relations with America, remembering that it is our main competitor and is not interested in Russia's prosperity and might. (*Rossiyskaya Gazeta*, 3.12.93)

Zhirinovsky seems to be convinced that the United States will offer no resistance when Russia starts to reclaim Alaska. And the reason for that is because it will perish of its own accord, just as the USSR has. (*New Times International*, October 1992)

Like a chameleon, Zhirinovsky is likely to adopt such attitudes toward the USA as are suggested by the mood of his country, as he perceives it. At the moment he is hostile because the general mood is hostile to America. He can be quite candid about this. President Clinton refused to meet Zhirinovsky during his visit to Moscow, so he tried to turn the snub to his advantage, declaring: President Clinton showed himself to be a weakling. This is a gift, as anti-American feeling is growing in Russia because the people know that Clinton supports the disintegration of Russia. (AP, 15.3.94) Zhirinovsky advised Clinton to go home to Arkansas and play the saxophone there. He added that the USA was clearly in a bad way and that under his leadership Russia would mount a massive aid effort to help it. He warned Clinton: Don't make the mistake Napoleon and Hitler made: withdraw from Europe (*La Stampa*, 16.12.93). And he offered further advice through Nixon: **Don't support the losers in the last elections. There is no future in it.** Another of his messages to Clinton was, he told reporters after his meeting with Nixon: **Don't be afraid of me. There is no reason to be afraid of my party.** The inscription in the copy of his own book that he asked Nixon to give to Clinton is: "**I don't want to be misunderstood by you.**" He criticized the United States for backing **radical democrats, who are all former Communists and are destroying the country.** (AP, 15.3.94)

Zhirinovsky has accused the Western powers of launching their third attack against Russia this century, the first two being the two world wars. **It was all the same to them who ruled Russia, tsars or Communists. Their goal was to destroy Russia. The country this time is being undermined by a peaceful invasion of pretty slogans about democracy and human rights . . . The Americans are clever. They know it is better to come here with chewing-gum, stockings and McDonalds.** (*The Vancouver Sun*, 9.4.94)

His prognosis for the USA is that some time in the next century its population will perish, swamped by blacks and Hispanics, and it will go the way of the USSR. He writes: **We will not gloat when California joins Mexico, when a Negro republic is created in Miami and when the Russians take back Alaska,** or when America dissolves into a **Commonwealth of New States** (*The New Republic*, 14.2.94). **The factories will close down. There will be no medicine, no food, and you Americans will emigrate to Europe, to Japan and to Russia.** (*La Stampa*, 16.12.93)

JAPAN AND ASIA

Zhirinovsky's plans about Japan are sometimes difficult to understand. Generally speaking, his stance is hostile without, however, directly threatening Japan. On the other hand, he wants to discourage aggression on the part of Japan. His general attitude may be summarized as follows: **Was Hiroshima and Nagasaki not enough for you? Do you want to have another nuclear holocaust? No? In that case forget about the Kurils.** (*New Times International*, October 92)

We won't give up a meter of land [on the Kuril Islands]. **We are ready to accept new land at the request of the masses. We will run out of border posts.** (*Warsaw Voice*, 20.3.94)

The Sea of Okhotsk between the Russian mainland and the Kurils should fall under Russian jurisdiction, and a 200-mile [320-kilometer] **protective fishing zone should be created. Not a single foreign ship will enter that sea, so that all the sea food will get on to the tables of the Russian people.** (AP, 13.12.93)

Zhirinovsky has proven willing to change his line on several key issues in his quest for power. The Kurils are a case in point. His firm stand against returning the islands was a major factor in his obtaining strong support in the December 1993 elections in the Russian Far East. However, in an interview with the *Wall Street Journal Europe* in 1990 he saw things differently. In those days he advocated a sweeping overhaul of Soviet foreign policy, including the realignment of various borders based on bargains and trade-offs. The Kurils were a problem for the Communists for ideological reasons but not for him and the LDPR.

Zhirinovsky was asked by an English reporter what he wanted to do about the Kuril Islands dispute in January 1993. **I would bomb the Japanese. I would sail our large navy around their small island, and if they so much as cheeped, I would nuke them . . . and we Russians haven't forgotten English treachery during the war. You're a small island, so you watch out, too.** (*Financial Times*, 14.12.93)

On relations with China: **We want it to develop its activity toward the south.** (*Warsaw Voice*, 20.3.94)

With Japan, Mongolia and China we have no territorial problems. (*Die Welt*, 29.1.94)

President Clinton is a coward. AIDS is a plague from the United States. If Germany and Japan don't stop harassing Russia, bombs will fall on their cities. (AP, 6.2.94)

CENTRAL AND WESTERN EUROPE

Zhirinovsky addressed two thousand activists of the far-right German People's Union (DVU) at a rally in the Bavarian town of Passau on 2 October 1993. The DVU, headed by German extremist Gerhard Frey, campaigns against foreign immigrants and for the reclamation of old German lands from Poland.

Our borders must shift closer together. Germany and Russia should again have a common border. . . . When I am in the Kremlin and one of you Germans looks askance at us Russians, you will pay for everything that we Russians have rebuilt in Germany. And the same goes for the Japanese. We will create new Hiroshimas and new Nagasakis. I will not drag my feet over using nuclear weapons. You know what Chernobyl meant for our country. You will get your own Chernobyl in Germany. (*Reuters*, 13.12.93)

On a visit to Austria in late December to meet a friend, former Carinthian timber merchant Edwin Neuwirth, Zhirinovsky gave his views on the future of Europe. **We have dissolved the Warsaw Treaty, but NATO continues to exist. NATO must also be dissolved. All foreign troops must be withdrawn. Europe must be shaped in the** same way as Austria. Austria might become the capital of the whole of Europe as a single country. German, Russian, English, French—that is all. (ORF TV, 21.12.93)

During his visit to Poland in early 1994 Zhirinovsky changed his tune about the fate of the country. This time he was polite and made no threatening remarks. In fact, he repudiated his earlier comments that the eastern part of Poland should be ceded to Russia. **I would not like anybody to think, even theoretically, that the Polish borders should be changed, ever; we are for a strong Poland, so that Russia and Poland can be good neighbors.** Zhirinovsky emphasized that Russia had no territorial claims and its army would never go west. However, he also declared: **Russia would not allow Poland to be used as a corridor for foreign aggression against Russia.** (MON, 12.3.94)

The so-called Oder–Neisse Line is not the last word in history. (*Frankfurter Allgemeine*, 16.12.93)

I am not threatening anyone, but I am warning everyone that if there is any danger to Russia, I shall harden my policies, said Zhirinovsky during his visit to Poland. **We took Berlin in 1945 and then gave it back again. Now the Germans live well and we do not. Why did we conquer Berlin then? We ought to have forced millions of Germans to work for us.** (*Frankfurter Allgemeine*, 16.12.93)

The opinion he is expressing here is reminiscent of the current Serb nationalist tenet expressed by Dobrica Ćosić, whom many see as the ideological mentor of Milošević, in his inaugural lecture at the Academy in 1977: "Serbs are victorious in wars and are defeated in peace." Another idea expressed by Ćosić reminds us again of Zhirinovsky: "Internationalism has destroyed the Serb nation."

The German magazine *Der Spiegel* ran a special issue about Zhirinovsky, which obviously pleased him for its publicity value. However, he objected to a couple of points. **My picture on the cover is very nice. But if I see my photograph next to Hitler's again, and if I am again compared to Hitler, then I see a bleak future for *Der Spiegel*. I can see it being wound up. We will sue *Der Spiegel* for damages to the tune of 100 million marks.** (*Der Spiegel*, 24.1.94)

The question of north Prussia and Königsberg [Kaliningrad] will in any case be solved in accordance with the wishes of Germany . . . The area of Königsberg must not be a bone of contention between Russia and Germany. (*Der Spiegel*, 51, 1993)

Gerhard Frey, a Munich businessman who makes no attempt to conceal his nostalgia for Hitler's Third Reich, runs a flourishing business selling Nazi memorabilia. He is a friend of Zhirinovsky, who visited him in December 1993. Herr Frey, publisher of a rightwing nationalist newspaper, *National-Zeitung*, constantly casts doubt on the existence of Nazi war crimes and promotes the rehabilitation of Hitler's *Wehrmacht* as the "best soldiers in the world." He wrote in the late December issue of his paper that if Zhirinovsky came to power, Russia would negotiate with Germany over the return of its lost province of east Prussia, which has been Polish and Russian territory since the end of the Second World War, when the Oder and Neisse rivers, hundreds of miles west of the east Prussian city of Königsberg, were established as Germany's eastern border. "The Russian Liberal Democrats offer negotiations over east Prussia and envisage a revision of the crying injustice of the Oder–Neisse Line through negotiations as a just solution," Frey wrote.

The area of Königsberg also belongs to Russia . . . One day we can return Königsberg to Germany. We want to give back everything the West wants. (*Die Welt* 29.1.94)

Germany does not really need foreign troops, and I cannot see any proper reason to have foreign troops stationed on the territory of the Federal Republic and, on the other side, to put German soldiers under foreign command. Germany is not a protectorate but an important power . . . I like to have a healthy military capable of the defense of Russia, and I also represent the interests of the army. No one can be more for peace than I. But it cannot be in the interests of Russia and Germany, and, for that matter, of almost the whole world, if Russia is deprived of power. Then the world will have to dance to the tune of the world policeman. (*Spotlight*, 7.3.94)

Zhirinovsky has a habit of making contradictory statements about the same subject. When his visa application was refused by the German consulate in Sofia, he threatened Germany with **stationing 300,000 Russian soldiers on German soil after coming to power.** He also told the perplexed German consular official that the **First World War started with the assassination in Sarajevo of the heir to the Habsburg throne. And you know how World War II came about?** He added that preventing him from going to Germany might lead to **World War III** (DPA, January 1994).

In reply to a question about the relations between Russia and the Nordic countries he replied: **There will be festivals, festivals and only festivals.** (*The Times*, 21.12.93)

THE MIDDLE EAST

The majority of mankind is interested in dissecting the Muslim world. The Muslim peril has to be eliminated. The Russian army's last march to the south would lead it to the shores of the Indian Ocean and to the Mediterranean and would mean liberation for 20 million Kurds, hundreds of thousands of Baluchis and Pushtuns. (*Los Angeles Times*, 4.3.94)

I like [Saddam Hussein] **as a person. Kuwait was to Iraq as Crimea is to Russia. Both should be back where they belong.** (*The Times*, 21.12.93)

Zhirinovsky's outrageous remarks are not accidental; they are the object of the exercise, or in any case were until he made a name for himself. He simply follows the principles of advertising.

We need close ties with the Arab states, including Iraq and Syria. (ITAR–TASS, 13.12.93)

Zhirinovsky made a speech to armed volunteers whom he sent to defend his hero, Saddam Hussein, in January 1993. **I wish you a safe return, though some of you may die there. You will die for a noble cause** (*Independent*, 25.1.93). Were these volunteers told, perhaps, that they would take part in a new Gulf War?

You are going to defend Iraq, a victim of reckless aggression by America and Israel . . . We will blow up a few Kuwaiti ports and aircraft, plus a few American ships in the Gulf. (*Financial Times*, 14.12.93)

Iraq? I'm the best friend of the Iraqi people. (*La Stampa*, 16.12.93)

Saddam Hussein invited me on one occasion. Had the Israelis done so, I'd have gone there too. (*Der Spiegel*, 51,1993)

I personally met Saddam Hussein . . . He listened to me, and asked questions. (*Guardian*, 7.1.94). This quotation from Zhirinovsky's book gives a good idea of the general style of that work, which, apart from some outrageous remarks, is written mostly in a somewhat pedestrian prose.

I have never sent volunteers to fight in Iraq. It was a cultural exchange: the boys went to see the museums in Baghdad. (*La Stampa*, 16.12.93)

Russia ought to be willing to **blow up a few Kuwaiti ports and aircraft, plus a few American ships,** to defend an old ally, Iraq. (*New Yorker*, 27.12.93)

Zhirinovsky's planned "dash to the south" would appear to involve a severe blow to the Middle East. **The break-up of the Muslim world will benefit most of humanity. It will also free Europe from the Israeli trap.** (*Guardian*, 7.1.94)

According to Zhirinovsky, Russia is losing its position in the Middle East, where **Iraq is its most reliable ally.** To the east and south Russia ought to be building relationships with Japan, China and India. **As for the allied relationship with India, it will depend largely on whether Russia helps it repel the Muslim threat.** In Zhirinovsky's view, access to the Indian Ocean should become a goal of Russia's foreign policy to the south. Afghanistan, Iran and Turkey would have to be "neutralized," which, according to him, **will be applauded in Europe.** (Zhirinovsky's statement to the press, INTER-FAX, 24.11.92)

Good relations continue between Zhirinovsky and Saddam Hussein. At the time of the LDPR's congress in April 1994 an official of the Iraqi Ba'ath party brought greetings from Hussein. Zhirinovsky sent his warm greetings to Baghdad in return and reiterated **his support for the just struggle being waged by the Iraqi people** (INA News Agency, Baghdad, 3.4.94). The wording of this message is very much in the Soviet style. Zhirinovsky does his best to distance himself from the Soviet period, and in his speeches he strikes a note that would have been quite alien to the official style of Communist politicians. But when it comes to formulas, he necessarily falls backs upon the only vocabulary he knows, just as everybody else in the country does. Vocabulary is the ballast that the new Russian politicians find most difficult to shed.

THE THIRD WORLD

I suggest that a different foreign policy, a radically different foreign policy, will be a source of money. Yesterday you learned from the mass media that Mengistu Haile Mariam fled from Ethiopia. This is a regime in which we invested billions. He fled—but who will return our billions to us? What will bring them back from Africa, from Latin America and from Asia? It is, after all, an impossible foreign policy to pursue. We invested billions, we got our people killed—and the regimes have collapsed. Some foreign policy! (Soviet Television, 22.5.91)

With Khrushchev the ideas of the Komintern poured out in a cascade. The Communist movement regained vigor. We put ourselves out to aid "the Egyptian brothers"; the Cuban saga commenced. Khrushchev tried to assume the functions of the pope of the Komintern, "to learn to live" with a billion Chinese. (*Le Monde*, 23.12.94)

FIVE

Russia

MOMENTS OF RUSSIAN HISTORY USED OR ABUSED BY ZHIRINOVSKY

Which are the events of Russian history that are still very much alive in the minds of present-day Russians and therefore influence political behavior? And which are the memories (real or imagined) that a demagogue can exploit because they have become more important since the demise of the Soviet Union, as the entire nation has been deprived of spiritual sustenance—something that Russians have always needed and have always been proud to need.

The Byzantine Moment

Russian nationhood, and the consciousness of it in particular, was founded on Prince Vladimir's conversion to the Greek Orthodox Christianity of Byzantium in the tenth century. As so often in Russian history, conversion was by force, with troops driving people into the rivers for mass baptism. By linking itself to Byzantium Russia joined Europe, inheriting Roman traditions but, in its case, those adopted by the eastern half of the Empire surviving 1453, when Constantinople fell to the Turks, Byzantium disappeared, and Russia assumed the role of the Third Rome. Russia formed its national character by borrowing Byzantine art (icons) and architectural features and the Cyrillic script modeled on the Greek alphabet.

The Nomadic Moment

As if in doubt about the best place from which to rule Russia and to defend it from attack, the Russians, like nomads, kept moving their capital around—it was first Kiev, then Vladimir, and, after an interval, Moscow by 1340, then it moved from Moscow to St. Petersburg between 1703 and 1715 and then, of course, back to Moscow in 1917. What provoked the original Russian people to commence their restless expansionism were the invasions by waves of nomadic Mongols from the ninth century onwards. The Russian state has encountered, from its inception, a variety of nomadic incursions (hostile or otherwise) along its southern frontier, but in the thirteenth century the invasion of the Mongols was an incomparably important experience, which is still, as it always has been, a source of trauma in the Russian psyche. The Tatar occupation and vassalage lasted for more than two centuries and developed in the Russians a sense of insecurity that has lurked in the collective mind ever since. The long struggle against the nomads and then against the Golden Horde, the state that the invading Tatars came to form, has bequeathed Russian folklore a series of mighty heroes and colorful events. For a while— perhaps for a very long while—the Tatar invasions cut Russia off from Europe and turned its face toward Asia. Scratch a Russian, goes the popular saying, and you find a Tatar.

Ivan the Terrible

That you become like your enemy is the oldest truism in psychology. The fact that Ivan the Terrible (1533–84) was the ruler to seize the last Tatar strongholds, Kazan in 1552 and Astrakhan in 1556, says it all. While suspicion, a craving for security, secrecy, sentimentality and savagery are the raw meat of the Russians' history, their soulfulness and saving-the-world messianism, inherited from Byzantium, are their all-embracing sauces.

The treatment meted out to the Russians by the Tatars was relayed and redoubled by the Russian nobles *vis-à-vis* the peasantry, who became serfs, yoked to one spot, virtual slaves working up to three days per week on the lords' fields and paying two thirds of the produce from their own land in tribute. The regime was far harsher than its equivalents in the West and harsher even than those of the slaves in the US South. It became generalized, as Ivan the Terrible favored the middling landowners against the greater, or *boyars*, whom he decimated. Indeed, he even denied them the right to travel. By the end of his brutal reign everyone in Russia could be deemed to be not only Slavs but also slaves, the derivation of the name.

The "Time of Troubles"

Ivan's death led after an interval to ten years of utter chaos, when no one seemed to know what path to take. Preceding this turmoil, and perhaps precipitating it, there was the famous figure of Boris Godunov, who is thought to have murdered the legitimate heir, Dimitri, to seize power. During the "Time of Troubles" several False Dimitris arose, aspiring to supreme power. Many people in Russia refer to the present period also as the "Time of Troubles."

Peter the Great

The most remarkable of the Romanov dynasty (1613–1917) was Peter the Great (1689–1725), giant in stature and quite tireless, who was determined to correct Russia's backwardness and drag it into the modern Western world by means of "shock therapy." Barbarism was to be rooted out—if necessary, by barbaric means. Western technological and cultural influence became paramount. The capital was shifted again, this time to a city that he founded, St. Petersburg, at the price of a million forced laborers' lives.

Peter the Great's forceful modernization was repeated early in the twentieth century by the Bolsheviks. Another attempt is now in progress.

Catherine the Great and Late Tsarist Russia

Catherine the Great (1762–96), wife of Peter III, whom she promptly usurped, surrounded herself with French and German luminaries in order to establish an enlightened despotism. The period stretching from her reign to 1917 was marked by a number of partial and sometimes aborted reforms, such as the emancipation of serfs in 1816, and by a great flowering of literature, the arts, science and mathematics. The invasion by Napoleon in 1811–12, which did not achieve its purpose, reinforced the Russians' age-old sense of insecurity and spurred them on to further conquests in order to secure their realm by adding even more buffer zones (see Chapter 2).

By the eve of the First World War Russia was in full economic up-swing, but this was not accompanied by a comparable development of civil society and political institutions (the Duma, or parliament, was convened, only to be dissolved by the tsar).

War and Revolution

The decision by the last tsar, Nicholas II, to participate in the First World War turned out to be an unmitigated disaster for the Russians. A new (reputedly half-German) leader appeared via Germany, Vladimir Ilyich Ulyanov—Lenin—in a new "Time of Troubles." A fanatical revolutionary, he borrowed a Western idea, Marx's Communism, in order to elevate Russia to a leading role not only in Europe but in the whole world. He set out to destroy the Russian heritage accumulated throughout the centuries. Instead of emulating the West, like Peter the Great, he hoped that this time the West would emulate Russia.

Stalin

But Russian history took revenge on Lenin's ideals. At his death in 1924 the obvious successor to him—victor of the Civil War, the highly cosmopolitan and resolutely internationalist Jew, Trotsky—lost out to a new despot whose career eclipsed that of the harshest of the tsars: Stalin.

His rule, spanning virtually thirty years (1924–53) brought quick industrialization, the transformation and destruction of a flourishing agriculture, an extensive network of forced labor camps (GULAG), a vast and well-equipped army and air force and a victory over a new invader: Hitler.

The period following the Second World War, which was meant to clinch the success of Russia as a leading power, did, indeed, bring victory and military parity with the USA. It resulted in the Cold War.

While the West thrived on the Cold War years, the Soviet economy was nothing but a military–industrial complex, with a highly trained work force, making unending sacrifices for a future to come, fed and served by a civilian economy that did not fulfill its early promise in the Khrushchev years. By Brezhnev's time the whole country had settled into a quite comfortable and increasingly corrupt stagnation. World supremacy was not to be.

Gorbachev–Suicide Trip

A new period of reform started with Gorbachev (1985–91), who thought that the Soviet Union's society and economy, however drab, could be made liberal-democratic and efficient (hence *glasnost* and *perestroika*). His attempt was marked by the final decline of the Soviet political élite: they had forgotten that the basis of their power was coercion and repression. Reforms have been the main issue in Russian society since the collapse of the Soviet Union, resulting in the loss of two buffer zones: the satellite states of Central Europe and the Soviet republics. Russian expansion, which continued under Stalin, was suddenly put into reverse; and the loss of vast areas, coupled with growing economic chaos and a population that is completely baffled by developments, has undermined the self-confidence of most individual citizens as well as the nation as a whole.

The Russians, trying to obliterate the memory of the Soviet era, are harking back to Russian nationalism, the Orthodox Christian world (savagely suppressed by the Communists) and dreams of a Russian empire that existed until the First World War. The Russian leadership seems no less bemused by the sudden changes that it is striving to bring about. However they ring the changes on reform, the economy continues to deteriorate—except for its one highly efficient sector, the mafias.

And now a self-assured demagogue, Zhirinovsky, has appeared on the scene to pander to the dreams and wish-projections of a population in despair.

RUSSIA: ITS PAST AND PRESENT GRANDEUR

When the Soviet Union still existed, it was axiomatic for Zhirinovsky to proclaim Soviet nationalist sentiments.

Imperialism and colonial policy are foreign notions. We have no such things here. It was normal for us to have colonies; it was good, it was right. (*New Times International*, February 1992)

Russia once saved the world from the Ottoman Empire by sending its troops to the south. Seven centuries ago we stopped the Mongols. We have saved Europe several times: from the south, from the east, from the north and from the center of Europe itself. The world

should be grateful to Russia for its role as savior. (*The Last Dash to the South*)

On 13 December 1993, the very day on which news came through of the stunning electoral victory of the LDPR, its leader was being interviewed on Serbian TV, Belgrade, by Jasmina Stamenić-Pavlović, who asked him: "How do you see the future of your country, and is there a danger of Russia falling apart?" Zhirinovsky replied: **Of course we wish to view the future with optimism. We wish to realize those slogans of which I spoke earlier; we want Russia to be a strong, powerful state. Realistically speaking, I think that these unstable times will go on for some time, this blood, this violence; however, I believe that, ultimately, we will reach the point at which the Russian people will calm down, the economy will recover and we will discard all these ideological scarecrows for which people are dying today. However, the coming years will be difficult, very difficult in every respect.**

Russia will do only what is foreordained and will fulfill its great historical mission: to liberate the world from wars, which always begin in the south . . . Otherwise Russia will be unable to develop, and will perish, and we will be crammed with nuclear stations and nuclear weapons that will destroy the whole planet. (*The Last Dash to the South*)

Zhirinovsky has been opposed to the Commonwealth of Independent States (CIS) from the outset. **The goals of the CIS will mean the death of Russia. Russia will simply perish. Not right away but gradually, over the next twenty to thirty years, as new groups decide to secede. The only remaining Russians will be street-cleaners, sanitation workers, truck drivers—everyone else will have broken away.** (TASS, 18.12.91)

My two years in the army [1970–72] were very useful to me. First, I got to know the army itself . . . I had quite a good knowledge of

the nationalities' problems before, but the Transcaucasus region was different from Central Asia . . . All Russia's problems are in the south. So until we resolve our southern problem we will not extricate ourselves from this protracted crisis, which will periodically worsen. *(The Last Dash to the South)*

Zhirinovsky has said that the LDPR is not anti-Communist and that it condemns not **ordinary members but corrupt leaders. All nine Russian leaders from Nicholas II** (1894–1917) **to the present day have damaged Russia, but the coming elections could reverse this. Russia is now being run by an alliance between corrupt officials and mafia elements** (Russia TV Channel, 23.11.93)

There was something good about tsarist Russia. There were merchants, there were courtiers, workers, civil servants. *(The Last Dash to the South)*

Give me a billion dollars and I will become president of Russia . . . "Never shall anyone humiliate the Russians" [on Zhirinovsky's posters]. *(Financial Times, 14.12.93)*

There will be no lonely women in my Russia . . . We can't send everybody into the streets to sell vodka, lighters and condoms. *(US News and World Report, 10.1.94)*

The Bolsheviks came to power during the night by using violence . . . and rape. The next stage, the Stalin period, was a period when members of a party were being eliminated by that same party. It was not a struggle between two or three parties; there was just the one party on which Stalin depended. And the best members of the party were being eliminated. Compared with sexual morality, this reminds one of the problem of homosexuality, where there are relationships between representatives of the same sex.

Let's take another period, the Khrushchev period. It was different from Stalin's period. He was always smiling. But mostly he was alone. As for the people, we did not feel any pleasure. One can compare this with the problem of masturbation, when a person satisfies himself alone.

As for the periods of Brezhnev, Cherneko and Gorbachev, these were times of political impotence. The leaders wanted to perform, but they could not. They proposed things but they could not achieve anything, just as in the case of physical impotence. (Russia TV Channel, 26.11.93)

PAST AND PRESENT INJUSTICES AND SUFFERING—
THE MISTAKES OF THE PRESENT LEADERSHIP

Mum worked in an institute cafeteria, and the lecturers would often tell her about the examinations and about how sorry they felt for the Russian kids. A Russian would give an answer and get a "2," and a Kazakh would give just the same answer and get a "4" . . . Under Stalin's regime we were a closed country. That was a good thing in some respects—for instance, we were almost completely free of venereal diseases. And the level of morality in general was high. (*The Last Dash to the South*)

The present reforms are being conducted at your expense. The leadership wants you to die as quickly as possible, and you are already doing this. Zhirinovsky went on to say that for Russians the death rate now exceeds the birth rate and that children are dying because vaccine factories in other republics are not providing vaccines . . . Today I wish mainly to address the older generation and, in particular, pensioners and veterans because they are the ones who are suffering the most. Chiefly they have been dealt a great psychological blow—they have the impression that they have lived their lives in vain, that everything has been bad, the Revolution, the war and everything they have done. Our party takes a different position. We do not blame the older generation for anything. On the contrary, we bow down to you and say to all of you that you have done well. You are leaving us a normal country, a good economy in principle, great cities, fine transport, fine science and culture. You did everything you could and now you have the right to a dignified old age. (Russia TV Channel, 23.11.93)

For decades you have been deceived, made fools of and stuffed full of a variety of dogmas. I shall represent all those who have received, and still receive in these terrible years, only 200 roubles and live in two-room apartments. You are made to do nothing but work—work so that those at the top get rich. If I do not win the election, I will not be the loser. You, the inhabitants of Russia, will be the losers (Soviet TV, election speech, 22.5.91). Zhirinovsky never misses an opportunity to hammer home the fact that his unhappiness, poverty, etc., were the same as that of the Russian common man. Another point he emphasizes is that self-pity, both in his case and in that of the Russian people in general, is justified. Self-pity and self-flagellation have for a long time been the two national psychological sports in Russia, as witnessed by nineteenth-century Russian literature. The Soviets wanted to do away with self-pity and put pride and confidence in its place. They succeeded to a certain extent, but as soon as it became clear that their pride and self-confidence were without real foundation, a large part of the population quickly reverted to their former psychological habits.

The Oslo *Aftenposten* reporter interviewing Zhirinovsky on 4 November 1991 said that when Zhirinovsky's monologues start to deal with the injustice done to the Russian people, he scales the heights. He gesticulates with his hands, and his words come like bullets from a machine-gun.

Talking to *Izvestiya* on 30 November 1993, Zirinovsky said: **Do you think the Soviet Union could have collapsed all on its own? It was the price our society had to pay for letting the Communists** stay in power in National Democrat disguise. There is certainly some conspiracy behind this process in the country. Don't tell me that the Soviet Union was degenerating and its economy was decaying. The situation was carefully planned as part of the strategy to destroy Russia.

Zhirinovsky was asked: "Who harbored and implemented this strategy?" Russia's rivals, who dream of destroying Russia, with its powerful economy, huge armed forces and scientific achievements. (*Izvestiya*, 30.11.93)

In Ankara the plans for a greater Turkish state have long since been prepared. Pan-Turkism threatens Russia, since it has a large Turkic-speaking, Muslim population and also a Persian-speaking one; that is a good inducement for Afghanistan, Iran and Turkey to move north . . . And Russia loses everything. The "great and talented" Turkish nation is worthy of living right in the center of the world, in the scented region, on the shores of six seas; the weak and powerless Russia, however, must perish. Is this foreordained in the history of humanity? No, that is not possible. (*Die Zeit*, 14.1.94)

There are specific geopolitical factors that have played a part in the development of the Russian soul. Russia is situated in bad climate zones, with bad neighbors. For 700 years there have always been wars . . . The Tatar yoke for 300 years . . . With Turkey alone, thirty wars. With others, dozens, hundreds of wars. That is why there is something animal-like about "Russianness." Our intention to tame that instinct is the central point of our program. That's why we need a strong army, so that no one should be in Russia's way. (*Soziologische Forschungen*, No. 7, 1993)

In the spring Boris Yeltsin's regime will collapse. Tens of millions of hungry and unemployed Russians will sweep him aside. Russia is moving toward total economic collapse. (Soviet TV, 31.5.91). This is a prophecy that he never stopped repeating but returned to

with renewed vigor in spring 1994, issuing dire warnings about a
new revolt against Yeltsin, similar to that of October 1993, but linking
it also with strong rumors about Yeltsin's worrying state of health.

**Why did the Soviet troops enter Prague on 9 May 1945? Why did
millions shed their blood? Today they insult us there. They have
erected a monument to Bandera; they have erected a monument
to SS men. What about our army and our older generation of
citizens? They are spat upon today. Why did they shed their blood?
The Russians are the most humiliated and insulted nation.** (Moscow
Radio, Home Service, 11.6.91)

**The Russians everywhere will become a national minority being
slowly annihilated. There will be a slow assassination of the Russian
nation because there is no purely Russian territory . . . the Russian
people will perish.** (*New Times International*, February, 1992)

He has consistently criticized the **inconsistent and passive stand of
Russia's ruling circles with regard to Iraq.** Zhirinovsky's group of
deputies will **raise the issue of lifting sanctions against Iraq and press
for a change in Russia's diplomatic policy, among others, within
the framework of the UN.** (ITAR-TASS report, Moscow World Service, 2.4.94)

In reply to the question of why the August 1992 *coup* failed, Zhirinovsky said: **That was no *coup d'état* in the proper sense of
the word. Two or three groups at the center of power were fighting
with each other. That's why the *coup* could not be planned and executed like a military operation. And that's why it failed.** (*Die Welt*,
29.1.94)

RUSSIA'S PRESENT POLITICAL AND ECONOMIC PROBLEMS AND HOW ZHIRINOVSKY PROPOSES TO REMEDY THEM: WHAT TO DO FIRST?

No Communists and no "Democratic Russia"—we must be just Russians, at last. (*Die Zeit*, 14.1.94)

Industry? We shall be obliged to manufacture and sell a lot of weapons. (*La Stampa*, 16.12.93)

I have a whole concept [for improving the living conditions of soldiers]: it consists in a plan for training, and in a plan for creating congenial everyday living conditions and in the use of armies abroad . . . Soldiers under contract for hard currency could perform tasks assigned by the world community. You will ask, where will you get the resources to implement such grandiose plans? What about the sale of weapons abroad? Why destroy our tanks and weapons and, in the process, become poorer and poorer. (*Krasnaya Zvezda*, 30.5,91)

We cannot permit alien religions to destroy the minds of the young generation of Russians. (*The New Republic*, 14.2.94)

There are many ways of improving the economic life of the country. Take taxes. Many of our traders suffer from them. When I say, "We must deal a blow against crime," I mean that only Russian citizens in possession of a license should trade in Russian territory. (Mayak Radio, Moscow, 8.12.93)

Intellectuals are not Zhirinovsky's favorite breed. In fact, he despises them as much as Hitler did. He knows that they will never support him, but he shrugs this off by saying: How many votes do they have? Indeed, Moscow intellectuals are against me. There are

100,000, 1 million, 3 million, 10 million of them. But I'll need a 55 million electorate. (*New Times International*, October 1992)

Millions of southerners will go home, and you will breathe freely. Because it is not so much commercial kiosks that irritate you as those inside them. When healthy Russian lads, from your regions, are standing there with honest Russian faces they are too ashamed to deceive you. For, you know, it is mainly aliens and fly-by-night southern *mafiosi* who are the swindlers, burglars, rapists and killers. (Mayak Radio, 8.12.93)

Russia's move to the south is primarily a defensive measure, a counter-measure, because today there is a threat from the south, from the direction of Teheran, which is constructing plans for the pan-Islamic seizure of vast territories, from the direction of Ankara, where plans for a greater Turkic state were prepared long ago . . . Nothing would happen to the world even if the entire Turkish nation perished, although I do not wish that upon it . . . The principle of division [within Zhirinovsky's Russia] will be purely territorial inside the country: *guberniyas,* oblasts, provinces . . . The blending of peoples as a result of the economy, the dominance of the Russian language and the Russian rouble, the dominant position of the Russian army as the most combat-capable; these are historical facts. We must ensure stability throughout our region for Russia and for the world community as a whole. (*The Last Dash to the South*)

New armed forces can be reborn only as the result of a combat operation. The army cannot grow stronger in barracks (*Die Zeit,* 14.1.94). In his book Zhirinovsky then goes on to describe how maintaining the army and extending Russia's frontiers will have all kinds of other beneficial effects: they will stimulate the economy, transport and communications, and at the same time it will be possible to transport raw materials and foodstuffs to help industry. Russia will become rich. There will always be enough people to work in industry as the people from the south migrate north in search of work. This particular daydream about the future of Russia is, no doubt, modeled on the migration of people to Western European countries in the period after the Second World War, first from the poorer south European countries and later from Turkey, North Africa and Asia. This combat operation envisaged for the army stands in stark contrast to other descriptions of how the dash to the south could be achieved peacefully; far from being forced, people in the south will gladly submit to Russia. **What is wrong with a state-controlled economy? It has its drawbacks, but why destroy it? A huge number of plants and *kolkhozes* are working and producing output that we all need.** (*The Last Dash to the South*)

We advocate the principle of a mixed economy: the public sector should not be artificially broken up, nor the development of the private sector speeded up. Let everything develop naturally. Equal opportunities should be created both in the public and in the private sectors. Let the collective forms of economic activity (collective and state farms, auxiliary enterprises and agrobusinesses) and private activity, in the form of farms, peasant households and farmsteads, exist in the countryside. (*Rossiyskaya Gazeta*, 3.12.93)

In Russia there will be order—but only our order. What's happening right now is the destruction of the nation . . . There will be a military *coup* here . . . the army's role will be to save the fatherland . . . The people are not satisfied . . . I will come to power. (*Time*, 17.2.93)

I think the pensioner will support us; he will be at peace. He will have a roof over his head. He will always have something to eat, something to wear . . . And it [i.e., Zhirinovsky's accession to power] will mean that some of the population will live very well because people will have the opportunity to work honestly and, after that, to enjoy a secure old age. Because there will be no more revolutions and *perestroikas* in our country, we will put an end to the uncertainty. The path to victory is the implementation of ideas via the success of the party and its leader. These are all interconnected . . . We need to hold elections, but free elections, so that everyone who wishes to can participate in them. The voters should decide how much each party is worth. Second, we need to adopt a very concrete program that is tied to the state. We have to prevent national divisions in Russia. There should be no Tataristan or Yakutia. Only territorial units should exist, as in every other country in the world. Third, we need to take a step back in the economy. We must strengthen the state sector, while in the private sector those who manufacture products should be given the chance to develop. We have to stop providing aid in every direction, in every respect, and we have to stop the conversion of the military industry. (*The Last Dash to the South*)

We must establish strong Russian borders. If someone owes us something and does not have the money to pay, we must confiscate their property. (Serbian TV, Belgrade, 13 12.93)

The frontiers of the USSR, recognized by the world community, as of 1975 will be restored, and Russian flags will fly over the cities of Kazakhstan, Central Asia, the Transcaucasus, etc. (ITAR-TASS, World Service Radio, 2.4.94)

Zhirinovsky emphasized during his 1993 election campaign that Liberal Democrat deputies in the Duma **will never allow Parliament to act in such a way that anyone could dissolve it or even raise the issue of disbanding it. Moreover, never again in the history of Russia will anyone dare to fire at parliament. We shall never allow such a monstrous act. Also, such a blasphemy as presenting awards and titles only two days after this vile victory** [the taking of the White House in October 1993] as a **reward for Russians killing Russians in**

the capital of Russia is, of course, terrible. (This particular turn of phrase, "is, of course, terrible," is a favorite with Zhirinovsky. In certain sections of his book it is a rhetorical *ostinato*. It may come off better in live speech—he is known to be quite an orator.) **We shall try to put right that mistake, to rescind these titles and awards. I think the recipients will themselves lay down these titles and awards.** (Moscow TV, Ostankino Channel, 17.12.93)

In the same TV address he promised that the Duma would **raise the question of releasing Aleksandr Rutskoy, Albert Makashov and Vyacheslav Achalov** (who took part in the defense of the White House in October 1993, although, perhaps significantly, he does not mention the name of the leader of the Parliament, Ruslan Khasbulatov, who is a Chechen) **from Lefortovo prison.** He quickly added, for effect, that **those who initiated** *perestroika,* **ruining our economy and destroying our state will be brought to book.** That was a promise he kept and successfully fulfilled in February 1994; he was present at Rutskoy's release from prison, took credit for it and announced: "The choice for president at the next elections is between Rutskoy and me."

Another promise of his, which President Yeltsin kept for him, was made in the same speech: **Boris Nikolayevich Yeltsin will often be on holiday . . . You'll see very little of him. Parliament will work very well.**

Zhirinovsky has always opposed the Commonwealth of Independent States on the grounds that it is harmful to Russian interests. **The goals of the Commonwealth of Independent States will mean the death of Russia. Russia will simply perish. Not right now, but gradually over the next twenty or thirty years, as new groups decide to secede.** (Zhirinovsky's press conference, as reported by TASS, 18.12.91)

Who will be our next president? The people must elect him. The choice is between me and Rutskoy (*Die Zeit*, 4.3.94), he said, after Rutskoy, one of the leaders of the rebellion against Yeltsin and his government in October 1993, was released from prison with an amnesty. That was a great humiliation for Yeltsin: he ordered the attack against the White House, defended by rebel parliamentarians, in order to have a parliament that he could control. The elections in December produced a new parliament against which he was as powerless as he had been against the previous one. That was predicted by Zhirinovsky, who on the night of the election said: **The moral and political climate in the country has turned against the state. No state in the world would permit the creation on its territory of such a large number of organizations with the declared aim of destroying that state. Nobody should allow this. Whereas democracy presupposes the existence of parties, newspapers, democracy appears also to assume the opposite process—banning parties and newspapers, not applying certain laws and introducing new laws. As we understand it, things can follow only one path—either everything is banned for decades, and nothing is permitted, and we all become serfs again; or else everything is permitted, and we have bacchanalia, anarchy, and nobody knows anything.** (Soviet Television, 22.5.91)

If I were president, with my first decree I would subordinate the armed forces to myself and put them on a state of military alert; secondly, I would give every officer military rank up to colonel, and I would also give them the right to obtain a car made in the fatherland. (TASS, World Service in English, 18.12.91)

There are no laws today. As the ancient Greek philosopher Plato said, long before Russia or Europe existed: "Any state where the force of law does not operate, where some force does not operate, will perish." And how we are perishing today. (Soviet Television, 22.5.91)

Decisive steps are needed. We must not cut the army and the Ministry of Security troops. We must get the officers' corps and the Ministry of Security to fight crime in the toughest way. We must allow, temporarily, field courts-martial to be organized. If a criminal group is caught red-handed, its leader must be shot and killed immediately, on the spot, and the members of the group must be sentenced to different jail terms within three days. Only such decisive measures which, of course, will be temporary—for six months—will enable us to get on top of crime. Otherwise it will get on top of us. (Mayak Radio, 8.12.93)

In this country today the words "soldier," "officer," have almost become swear words. It is absolutely necessary to save the army from indiscriminate criticism, to create the best material conditions for servicemen. (*Krasnaya Zvezda*, 30.5.91)

The conversion of factories to civilian production must be stopped. The military–industrial sector must again produce submarines, which, when exported, will earn us $200 million apiece . . . In Russia there will be order—but only our order. What's happening right now is the looting of the nation. (*Time*, 17.2.93)

I will immediately declare a dictatorship—the country cannot afford democracy for now. I will stabilize the situation in just two months. (*Time*, 27.12.93)

I shall put all the strikers behind bars, train the racketeers and send them abroad to defend our national interests there, bring in cheap manpower from abroad and compel [the labor force] to work like hell for a hundred roubles a month. (*New Times International*, February 1992) (Another instance of "their order" and of playing to a gallery unaccustomed to the nuisance caused by strikes to the public—strikes were unheard of in Soviet times.)

If I come to office next April, of which I have no doubt, in May those who signed the agreement at the creation of the CIS in Alma Ata will be in prison charged with staging a *coup d'état* . . . For some reason Russians are not supposed to have their own state, where they are born, where they live, where their forebears died and where they founded cities. (TASS, 8.1.92)

Zhirinovsky's party, the LDPR: **The people elected the party for the sake of stability.** (Speech in Belgrade, 30.1.94, as reported by Tanjug). As for trade with Russia: **Whoever wants to export goods to Russia must first send us what they wish to sell. If they are good, we will pay. Whoever wants to buy our goods must pay first, and then we will dispatch the articles paid for** . . . What about banks? **I have nothing whatever to do with banks.** (*La Stampa*, 16.12.93)

In one of the few remarks he has made about parliamentary alliances he stated that he **wants to have links with the Women of Russia party,** which is regarded as being part of the "communist block." (*La Stampa*, 16.12.93)

I will raise up Russia—Russia that is now prostrate . . . **I dream of the day when Russian soldiers can wash their boots in the warm waters of the Indian Ocean.** (*Frankfurter Allgemeine*, 16.12.93)

His plans when he gets into power: **5,000 gangs will be eliminated in Russia.** (*Frankfurter Allgemeine*, 14.12.93)

In reply to a question about how he is going to fulfill his promise to feed the nation in seventy-two hours: **It is very simple, really: I shall order 1.5 million troops into the former GDR, brandish arms there, nuclear arms included, and there'll be enough food to go around.** (*New Times International*, October 1992)

Words like "republic," "autonomy," must go . . . There should be forty or fifty regional units in Russia; the central government must concentrate on questions like foreign policy, finance, defense, transport, communications, energy supply, ecology. (*Der Spiegel*, 51, 1993)

The political system of Russia will soon receive first aid in the form of the LDPR . . . The mighty vessel of the LDPR has set sail on the expanses of the oceans, and all unseaworthy tubs have been left behind. (ITAR-TASS report, Moscow Radio World Service, 2.4.94)

THE FUTURE: ZHIRINOVSKY'S RUSSIA

Just before the December 1993 parliamentary elections, in a television program, Zhirinovsky outlined how he sees the future of Russia and what kind of state it is going to be under him. The state, he said, is essentially the treasury and the army. If the treasury is empty and there is no army, then there is no state. The treasury is empty because it has been robbed by those who are seated before you today and ask with horror, "How can it be that our state has collapsed? How can it be that our economy has collapsed?" But it is they who have done this, all of them except our party . . . Television will be different, he announced. We shall ban all commercial advertisements. They will be allowed only in the newspapers. There will be no sneakers, no chewing-gum, no beaches. We have eight months of winter. We need fur coats and not . . . beaches and cooling drinks. You will be able to watch good Russian films. Ninety percent of all news on our television channels will be about Russia, in the good Russian language. You will be spoken to by Russian presenters with good, kind, blue eyes and fair hair. This can all be done quickly. (Moscow TV Ostankino, Channel 1, 7.12.93)

He clearly wants an economy—perhaps some form of market economy—but without the irritation of consumer desires. He does not want people to be goaded into buying things, which he finds intrusive, disturbing to the minds of ordinary citizens. His dream of a market economy is of one with a human face, without commercial pressure and the consequent social pressure. He promises the "human face," if not in so many words, in every field. His plans are for Russian expansionism with a human face: **The sound of bells of Russian Orthodox churches on the shores of the Indian Ocean and of the Mediterranean will bring peace to those peoples.** (*La Stampa*, 16.12.93)

How do I see Russia? I do not see Russia weeping . . . I see a proud Russia, a Russia wherein the glorious traditions of its army will once again be realized, where talented Russian engineers and industrialists will provide examples of the latest technology . . . We have a huge number of inventors, rationalizers . . . Russian mercantile traditions must be restored . . . This is how I see Russia. It will have the world's strongest army, strategic forces, missiles with multiple launchers. Our space-combat platforms, our "Buran" spaceship and "Energiya" rockets: these are the country's rocket shield . . . We have no rivals . . . Russians, a proud people; the twenty-first century will belong to us despite everything. In the next seven years we will finally put an end to all revolutions, all the *perestroikas*. We will put an end to Yeltsinism and Burbulisism. And we will enter the twenty-first century changed and pure . . . We must pacify the south for ever, so that there are vacation centers, youth camps, sanatoria and preventive treatment centers there on the shores of the Indian Ocean and the Mediterranean Sea . . . A single economy and a single legal and political structure would create favorable conditions for the development of all trades and for the culture, education, life and family structure that everyone wants. (*The Last Dash to the South*)

The division into spheres of influence continues. The main danger to Russia is concentrated in the south today. All our troubles have always originated, and will continue to originate, from there. The south is a highly unstable region—fire-spitting, controversial, riotous. Its future promises us conflicts and wars that would make **Dushanbe and Sukhumi** [the Tadjik and Georgian civil wars] **look like child's play. We must calm this region down; and the world community will ask us to do so.** (*Izvestiya*, 30.11.93). This will be carried out by a revived Russian army, **the final division of the world by means of shock therapy—suddenly, quickly, effectively.** (*The New Republic*, 14.2.94)

The fact that I have never been a Communist is the reason for my success in the elections. (Ostankino Channel 1 TV, 13.12.93)

I promise to adopt measures to put an end to the anti-Communist bacchanalia in particular regions and particular areas—within the framework of the law, of course. This anti-Communism should not be permitted. We are leaping from one extreme to another. Communism—we are all, so to speak, for this, but now there is a section of the population who are anti-Communists. The words "Russian" and "Communist" have now almost become insults. "Officer" likewise has become an insult. That cannot be permitted. (Soviet Television, 22.5.91)

As a flexible politician, he wants to please everybody, to be all things to all men—even the Communists. **To save Russia we will definitely abandon narrow party interests and are ready to form blocs with any force.** (*Independent*, 15.12.93). He manifests too great a readiness for political alliances to inspire confidence. With his characteristic and almost disarmingly candid disregard of niceties he indicates clearly that it does not matter with whom he is to join forces, since they will not be around for long once he has got into power. Is his abrasiveness toward other political figures and forces based on the calculation that whoever is in an influential position now will soon disappear from the political scene, and that his constituency is the only important factor in his type of direct "democracy"? Or is his style the result more of taste than of calculation—that is, is he really spontaneous and authentic, and is that his advantage over his rivals?

The Russian people have three choices. We can choose what we have now by voting for Gaidar and Yavlinsky, which will not suit many people, or we can choose to go backwards by voting for the Communists, which also does not suit many people. My party represents the third choice . . . Less democracy! More economy! That is our slogan. Look at China. I admit it was not very democratic to use tanks against the students, but the main thing is that the country itself still exists. And they do not have shortages of food and medicines, as we have . . . "You will be fine with me." (Campaign slogan) I am waiting in the wings. My moment has nearly arrived. (*Financial Times*, 14.12.93)

Boris Yeltsin is occupying my place only temporarily. I have already won. (*The Times*, 17.2.92)

The Turkish "democratic" way, which made it possible for the Turks to spread everywhere in Europe, is much worse for us. It is Kominternism, whereas fundamentalism is nationalism (*Le Monde*, 23.12.93). He does not like Kominternism because he identifies it with internationalism, which is, as he puts it, like living in a communal apartment with common bathrooms, whereas nationalism is like living in a self-contained apartment, where you are safely behind doors and you admit only such visitors as you choose. (See also Chapter 6.)

POLITICAL FIGURES AND RIVALS

Khrushchev . . . had absolutely no education in the humanities . . . Andropov too was an uneducated person. so all Russia's rulers have lacked a classical education . . . even Lenin . . . I realized that these dull-witted, sometimes simply stupid, people reached the heights thanks merely to the system that allowed them to do so. (*The Last Dash to the South*)

With Khrushchev the ideas of the Komintern poured out in a cascade. The Communist movement regained vigor. (*Le Monde*, 23.12.93)

Zhirinovsky's party was, from its earlier days in March 1990, organized on a broad scale, a fact that fed suspicions that he had special finance from the existing organs of power, notably rogue elements in the KGB. **Local party branches have been formed on the entire territory of the Soviet Union, from the Kamchatka peninsula to Moldova. The party has announced its existence in all the countries where liberal parties are available, that is, in about forty countries. In fact, the party has entered into contracts with practically all liberal parties. We have formed our political image as a moderate party of the centrist trend, seeking no social upheavals.** (Moscow Radio, World Service, 18.4.91)

Zhirinovsky made the point in the June 1991 election campaign that, at forty-five, he would be Russia's youngest president. **The bad old days of gerontocracy. How do Russia's new leaders differ from the old ones? They enjoy the same old privileges . . . Once again there is total deception, and they are making fools of you.** (Soviet Television, 6.6.91)

Zhirinovsky claimed that the West is supported by democratic Russia and that the government, **who are fulfilling Western orders and embezzling, do so less because of a tendency toward corruption than because they realize that they will not remain in power long.** (INTERFAX report on Zhirinovsky's speech, 7.5.92)

Russia's Foreign Minister [Shevardnadze] **was not a Russian. He is now the leader of a different state.** [Georgia]. **That's why he was in such a hurry to withdraw our troops from everywhere and to sign all those treaties, of no use to us; they were anti-state and anti-Russian in nature. He wanted an opportunity to pull his republic out of the USSR and become its leader.** (Russia TV Channel, Moscow, 26.11.93)

Boris Yeltsin is occupying my place only temporarily. I have already won. (*Time*, 17.2.92)

Zhirinovsky is often accused of being a Fascist. But he actually hurls the charge of Fascism at a great number of his political rivals, by implication not even exempting Yeltsin himself. In 1991 Zhirinovsky alleged that, when abroad, Yeltsin failed to visit Soviet war memorials. This has been denied by a representative of Yeltsin, who asked Zhirinovsky to apologize. Zhirinovsky's apology was as follows: **Wherever Yeltsin is there is war. There is Fascism. There is counter-revolution.** (Soviet Television, 6.6.91). Yeltsin's representative replied: "I am horrified at what will happen to Russia if such a president is elected." Zhirinovsky repeated that a Yeltsin victory would generate civil war in Russia and soon a military coup, the latter half of which prediction was borne out two months later, in August 1991. Zhirinovsky was asked what post he would like in a future government if he were defeated. **If the winner is not Boris Nikolayevich Yeltsin, I'll occupy the post . . . I am an international-affairs specialist by profession. I am prepared to occupy the post of Russian Foreign Minister and will ensure a totally new direction for Russia's foreign policy.** (Soviet Television, 6.6.91)

Komsomolskaya Pravda's representative invited Zhirinovsky, during the June 1991 election campaign, to name just one person other than himself in whom the country could believe. **Let the Russian people show through free elections in whom they wish to believe,**

Zhirinovsky replied. Yeltsin, he claimed, was avoiding face-to-face debate with him. **Let everyone's medical records be on public display. Let everyone see the parlous state of Yeltsin's health.** (Soviet Television, 6.6.91)

Yeltsin, he said, had the press in his pocket, along with an endless flow of finance for his campaign. **I'm starting to go sour. I need an enemy, somebody to fight with. The Communists and the democratic Russians are lying down—who can I fight with? I can't kick a man when he's down, understand? There is nobody to fight.** (NTV, Moscow, 29.3.94). Hitler thought that the political leader of genius could identify a good enemy to give his followers: The art of leadership consists of consolidating the attention of the people against a single adversary and taking care that nothing will fragment this attention. The leader of genius must have the ability to make different opponents appear as if they belonged to one category *(Mein Kampf)*. Mao Tse-Tung would not have agreed with Zhirinovsky's chivalrous sentiments concerning not kicking a man when he is down. As Mao said, there is absolutely no better time to do it. **The elections of 12 June are not free. They are elections for just one person. It is just another political comedy.** (Soviet Television, 6.6.91)

In the same election a correspondent of the newspaper *Kuranty* asked Zhirinovsky why he had said in an interview that, if he became president, he would allow a Fascist party to be formed, with the implication that he would be its Führer. **I'll answer in the way that I, a republican presidential candidate, want to . . . Today there are very many parties that do not bear the name "Nazi"—the popular fronts and so on—but whose actions are, precisely, Fascist and Nazi . . . I am a fierce opponent of Fascism, but today Fascism and the ground for it are prepared by such papers as *Kuranty*.** (Soviet Television 6.6.91)

After the December 1993 parliamentary elections, his attitude seemed to have softened toward Yeltsin. **Boris Nikolayevich [Yeltsin]** has changed lately. He is drawing closer to patriotic forces; he is identifying with Russia more openly. In that past few years his own staff have led him, again and again, into error—advisers like Gaidar, Burbulis, Chubais, Kozyrev. He himself did not want all the things that we have experienced as very negative. (*Der Spiegel*, 51, 1993).

He is good to me: he reads a page of my book every day. (*La Stampa*, 16.12.93)

Yeltsin has no conceptions. He is like a doctor who has put on a white apron and plans to operate but has no medicine and no ideas. You don't need a big brain to break up collective farms. They [the Democrats] are destroyers. Other forces are needed for creative purposes. We—our party—can provide such forces. We will sell weapons and will not shy away from this fact. Two whole years—in two whole years the Democrats managed to sell only two diesel-powered submarines. (*Kuranty*, 16.12.93)

After meeting us, he [Yeltsin] is now moving in our direction. He has amended his foreign policy and removed some anti-Russian elements from the government: Burbulis and Gaidar. (*Warsaw Voice*, 20.3.94)

Everybody is dropping Yeltsin. Not me . . . When things get bad I'll take a bag, put a few apples in it and buy a bottle. And when we've had a drink or two I'll ask him: "Boris Nikolayevich, why didn't you join me for a TV discussion before the elections?" (*Die Zeit*, 14.1.94)

I am not a Fascist. On the contrary, I have always made efforts in the struggle for human rights. Throughout my life I have not allowed myself a single extremist sortie. Some people even accuse me of being too soft toward Communists, but I am confident that the solution of all political disputes should be entrusted to the voters, to their verdict. (ITAR-TASS, 13.12.93)

It would be nice for the LDPR to cooperate with the political movement "Women of Russia"—gentle, neutral [and regarded by many as allied to the Communists]. (Russia TV Channel, Moscow, 12.12.93)

Gorbachev: He destroyed the country. (*La Stampa*, 16.12.93)

Gorbachev should go back to where he came from, to his village near Stavropol, where he was once sitting at the wheel of a tractor. (*Der Spiegel*, 51,1993)

Gorbachev's political ideas resulted in the state's and the economy's collapse. He should have introduced reforms in a different way. He should have made use of the existing power structures of the Communist Party, especially the KGB, and through just those structures carry out the democratization of the economy in the first place and then, as a second stage, the democratization of politics. (*Die Welt*, 29.1.94)

Yakovlev can retire to Canada, where he was ambassador for many years . . . And Schevardnadze? He will go on being the commander of the besieged city of Tiflis until one day he gets a bullet in his forehead, fired by a Georgian patriot. (*Der Spiegel*, 51, 1993)

THE ARMY

What an army needs is armed conflict, both inside and outside the country. Only wars will revive the Russian army. (*Economist*, 18.12.93)

If I don't rule, then no matter, let the military. In any case, they would be better than Yeltsin's democrats. (*Financial Times*, 14.12.93)

If I were president with my first decree I would subordinate the armed forces to myself and put them on a state of military alert. (TASS, World Service in English, 18.12.91)

A key theme in his pre-election campaign was the need to strengthen the Russian army (which may explain why so many soldiers, including, apparently, the Taman division, which played a key role in putting down the October rebellion in Moscow, appear to have voted for him). In 1991 Mr. Zhirinovsky won the nickname "the Nuclear Robin Hood," on account of a proposal to use the army to feed his hungry compatriots. How? **By sending nuclear armed troops into the former East Germany. They would come back with enough food to go round.** (*International Herald Tribune*, 7.3.94) He also advocates that the army deport millions of southerners— code for Caucasians and Central Asians—from Russia. He argued in a pre-election broadcast that field courts-martial should be organized to shoot criminal gang leaders on the spot. **This would allow local Russian lads, with honest Russian faces, to take over from the southerners as kiosk owners and market tradesmen.** (Stephen Mulvey, Vladimir Wolfovich, *Zhirinovsky: A Portrait*, p. 1).

After I become president, I shall place the army on high combat alert. Bandits from national armed units who do not hand in their weapons within seventy-two hours will be shot. (TASS, 8.1.94)

I do not rule out the use of our armed forces under the United Nations flag, for large payments in foreign currency, in different parts of the world, as is being done today by the multi-national forces in the Near East and as may happen in Africa. A foreign policy of that sort would be profitable. We put everything into Iraq, and Iraq was smashed, and we have now lost everything. We would not invest in anyone, but we would be ready to make available our valiant armed forces so that, in fulfilment of UN resolutions, they could be used somewhere as a sort of police force. (Soviet Television, 31.5.91)

Our party believes that all the combat operations that have been carried out by the tsarist army, the Soviet army and the present Russian army are justified. They have all been in accordance with the military doctrine of our Russian state, and all those who were decorated deserved their awards. So one may, with honor and dignity, wear decorations received under the tsar, under the Communists and under the present regime, since the army must stand aside from the political course of the grouping that is temporarily in power. It performs its sole duty, that of protecting the fatherland. (Russia TV Channel, Moscow, 24.11.93)

Wherever our soldiers have been—in the Soviet-Finnish War, in Afghanistan or in any other region, in Africa, in Cuba—they have done everything correctly. All the officers who fought, all the things that they did, were lawful. It was all correct, and they should always receive the necessary recognition from citizens . . . I should very much like to see a return to the time when civilians stood aside if an officer was walking along the street, and I should like people to look respectfully at an officer of the new Russian Volunteer Army. He, and even more his family, should never want for anything. We do not want Russian officers and men to be used anywhere as cannon fodder. If there is a need for them to take part in armed conflict, then we may provide military and technical assistance, but only on a contract basis and at a high price, and we may sell our equipment very dearly. The requesting nation must pay for the Russian equipment to demonstrate the greatness . . . and the power of Russian military thinking and the potential of Russian military factories . . . I have paid great attention to the military profession, and I will say candidly that, ever since I was a child, I have nurtured the tenderest feelings for our army as a state institution, regardless of the uniform. My grandfather—Pavel Ivanovich Makarov—was a soldier in the tsarist army and he wore a uniform. I don't know whom he supported, Reds or Whites, but the uniform was that of the old tsarist army. I was myself an officer in the Soviet army and served the two years in the Caucaus. But in what army will my son be an officer or an ordinary soldier? How are we to nuture patriotic feelings if a grandfather, father and son serve in different armies, in different uniforms, with different emblems? It's monstrous. In that sense it's hard for us to bring up the younger generation and harder even to do so in a patriotic spirit. (Russia TV Channel, Moscow, 24.11.93)

Zhirinovsky claims that Russia had developed a new secret weapon, the Elipton, which kills people by eradicating their brains. He claims to have tested this weapon in Bosnia on fifteen Bosnian Muslims who are all now dead. He also announced his intention to conduct further trials of the weapon in the Belorussian city of Brest, although no report has so far emerged of his having done so. He boasts of the weapon that it is purely ecological. It destroys opponents without leaving any contamination. (*Warsaw Voice*, 20.3.1994)

THE LIBERAL DEMOCRATIC PARTY OF RUSSIA

Neither I nor our party have ever given any support to the present political regime. This is a hundred-percent guarantee that we are different. (Mayak Radio, Moscow, 8.12.93)

We do not want to be supported by any particular group in society. In our party there are workers, company directors, students, members of the Academy, soldiers, generals . . . We do not believe in being oriented toward any class. (*Die Zeit*, 14.1.94)

We are the main party in opposition to the existing regime, he declared triumphantly, having received practically dictatorial powers from his party at the party congress (ITAR-TASS, Moscow Radio, World Service, 2.4.94)

We are in favor of a market economy, but one that would not strike a blow at the majority of our citizens, the state sector and the military–industrial complex . . . Let military plants . . . turn out market products; let them continue to sell. These plants should be converted gradually to peaceful production when the foreign market is saturated and they stop buying weapons . . . The foreign market demands weapons. (Zhirinovsky's campaign statement, TRUD, 11.6.91)

I represent the party that won Russia's first free elections. Our party came first. The Russian people elected this party knowing that it was the party of a new Russia, the party of a new foreign policy, the party of cooperation with the Serb people. (His speech in Bjeljina, reported by Tanjug, Belgrade, 31.1.94)

Our stance is firm: we are against the Soviet Union, against the CIS; we are for a mixed economy without the destruction of the state sector either in the cities or in the countryside; we are against the dissolution of *kolkhozes*. We are for defending all Russians and for secure borders. All the mafias that originate in the south must be eliminated: all Russian cities must be cleansed of them. A terrific blow must be dealt against crime. That is what we proclaimed in our manifesto, and that is still valid. (*Der Spiegel*, 51, 1993)

I say it quite plainly: When I come to power, there will be dictatorship [said during his 1991 presidential campaign.] (*AP*, 18.3.94.)

In the same speech he stated that he might **have to shoot 100,000 people, but the other 300 million will live peacefully.**

Some 22,000 billion roubles [$13 billion] are not being used in Russia today. Let the money be used by political forces interested in developing the country. It is unreasonable for you to invest in your needs or in the needs of one or two ailing or old men. That's not how you'll save the country (AFP, 15.3.94). This was said during a meeting with banking officials. At the time he was, or wanted to give the impression of being, short of funds, and he appealed to them for subsidies. With this request he may simply have wanted to reinforce his earlier assertion that his party is supported by ordinary citizens.

Asked about party funds: **We have more than 1 billion roubles in our party treasury. It all comes from simple people: contributions of 5,000, 10,000, 50,000 roubles arrive daily. You can check it at the main Post Office. Not a single rouble comes from shady sources . . . The world does not need to be afraid of us. There will never be any danger for others from Russian soil: no territorial claims, no military occupation, perfect observance of international treaties. Russia will be a civilized European country, open to the world, without any GULAG, without repression or Stalinism, or— God forbid—Fascism. Only democracy . . . We are against the Communists, just as we are against the ruling block. Russia's Choice. But we have nothing against allying ourselves in coalition: they can have two or three smaller ministries—at most.** (*Der Spiegel*, 51, 1993)

In the cities, where the more cultured, better educated, more prosperous classes live, we will not do so well. But in small cities, the rural areas of Russia, among the poor, among the young, among the military personnel, we will be supported (*Financial Times*, 9.12.93). He was proved right in that publication. From the very

117

beginning he has staked his political success on the vast rural expanses of Russia and on the support of the poorer sections of society or on those who have had little to expect from the reforms. In 1992, in reply to a statement of Alexander Yanov, **It is easy to make such promises to people. There is an enormous lumpenized mass which will buy them** (referring to Zhirinovsky's promises of quick economic upturn, the re-establishment of Russia's prestige and the elimination of corruption and gangsterism) he said, laconically: **It will buy them all right.** His clearsightedness verges on the cynical, something of which he is not in the least ashamed. When Yanov pointed out that the nation is, after all, not composed of lumpens alone and that lots of people retain common sense, he replied: **They do, they will vote against me, but they will be in the minority.** So does he bank on the degradation of the masses? **I most certainly do!** he declared. (*New Times International*, October, 1992)

The same political force is still in power. Its name is the Russian Social Democratic Workers' Party [the pre-revolutionary party that split into Bolsheviks and the less extreme Mensheviks]. **But its Bolsheviks won in October 1917 and the Mensheviks have won now. If you want real changes, you should vote a new political party into power. Out of nine parties, the only new one, the only one with an untarnished record, the only party with clean hands and a clear conscience—we are unsullied and unmarked by a single drop of blood—is the Liberal Democratic Party of Russia** (Russia TV Channel, 23.11.93).

Menshevik means minority, whereas *bolshevik* means majority. This did not stop Lenin from calling his party Bolshevik, even though his faction was in the minority at the last congress of the Russian Workers' Social Democratic Party in 1903. Lenin would have thought that he was in the majority morally because he was right and the other faction was wrong. This way of calculating majorities was exhibited by a later Bolshevik leader, Nikita Khrushchev. In

1959 he lost a crucial Presidium vote. He simply took the matter to the Politburo, the highest organ of the Soviet state, and overturned the decision. When somebody complained that this was not constitutional because the opposing side were in the majority in the main forum of the Presidium, where it was appropriate for the decision to be taken. Khrushchev replied: That was purely a numerical majority.

There are nine political blocs—I am referring to political parties—and eight of them are headed by members of the former ruling CPSU [the Communist Party of the Soviet Union]. All eight. There is one exception—the Liberal Democratic Party of Russia. As its chairman, I am sitting here before you. It is the only one. (Russia TV Channel, Moscow, 23.11.93).

The LDPR treasurer and number two in the party, Viktor Kobelev announced on 16 February 1994 that he was quitting the parliamentary faction of LDPR, then said that he and Zhirinovsky had ironed out their differences, although he admitted that their relations remained troubled (UPI, 17.2.94). On Kashpirovsky: **He was never in our Party. He made a statement** [not to represent the party in Parliament] **under the influence of Zionists and Ukrainian nationalists** (*Warsaw Voice*, 20.3.94). Anatoli Kashpirovsky, a well known faith healer and hypnotist in Russia, was elected as an LDPR deputy to Parliament in December 1993. He has since left the party to be an independent, along with Kobelev and three other LDPR deputies. Much as Zhirinovsky wishes to distance himself from the Communist period, having been brought up in it, he is permeated by Soviet methods, such as the retrospective amendment of history. The second part of Zhirinovsky's statement also needs interpretation. He was making a vague slur: Kashpirovsky is a Ukrainian Jew. This was probably in response to a private reference by Kashpirovsky to the widely held view that Zhirinovsky himself is a Russian Jew.

SIX

Zhirinovsky on Zhirinovsky and the World

Zhirinovsky's past life is a subject upon which he has pronounced at length in his book, *The Last Dash to the South*, and elsewhere. Before assessing his party and explaining how it was created, a brief account of his career up to that time will help to explain how such a relatively obscure figure in 1989 has been able to take advantage of the new Russian polity that has arisen out of the débris of the Soviet Union to further his keen ambition to preside over his country's future.

Born in Alma-Ata, capital of Kazakhstan, in 1946, he had a Russian mother and, in all probability, a Russian-Jewish father. Wolfovich, his patronymic, derives from Wolf, a common Jewish name. He admits that the name Wolfovich "sounds strange to Russian ears." He denies being half-Jewish, which, in a country where anti-Semitism is rife, is what he would be likely to do. The Kazakh authorities claim that his father's name on his birth certificate was Eidelshtein. But Zhirinovsky also denies this. It is known that he applied for an Israeli passport at one point in the mid-1980s and that his application was accepted. He did not take it up as a new opportunity came his way. There is also evidence of his having attended meetings of Shalom, a Jewish cultural organization founded in 1989;

he became the head of several of Shalom's committees, the other members of which took it for granted that he was as Jewish as themselves.[1] He takes pains to point out that he is not Jewish and also makes remarks which have a decidedly anti-Semitic ring to them. True, he couches them as merely anti-Zionist, but for decades "anti-Zionism" was simply the Soviet code word for anti-Semitism.

In *The Last Dash to the South* he describes at length his unhappy childhood, in a family of four, living in one room (where Zhirinovsky himself was born). His father was killed in a car accident. Then, at the age of four, his life was made worse when his 38-year-old mother took as a live-in lover a loutish 23-year-old technical student. Zhirinovsky claims that no one celebrated his birthday until he was 12. He also claims that when he was 2 or 3 he was forced to board at the home of a child-care provider.

At the age of 17, in 1964, he managed to enter Moscow's prestigious Institute of Oriental Languages, where he graduated in Turkish, which is one of four foreign languages he knows, the others being French and, rather less well, German and English. He describes these years as lonely ones, having been a poor provincial among his probably more polished fellow students. He admits to several abortive sexual experiences, which may have increased his penchant for brooding and self-pity.

In subsequent years, especially when he set out to follow what he describes in his book as his destiny to become a big-time politician, he made a point of stressing his sense of isolation and his self-pity, both in Alma-Ata and in Moscow, well aware of the prevalence of these traits in the Russian population at large. Like every Russian male, after graduating from the Institute he completed the usual two years of military service, in his case in the Caucasus, a particularly sensitive posting for a Russian soldier. He may have conceived his suspicion and dislike for Caucasians in general during these years. He graduated as a Soviet army officer, of which he remains inor-

[1] *International Herald Tribune*, 7 March 1994, p. 1.

dinately proud. It was during this period that his fascination with all things military was stirred: **I love the army,** he says.

He also declares his love for the KGB. And at this time it is quite possible that his love took a practical shape. Most students at the Institute, and many officers in the old Soviet days, were approached by the KGB to act as informers. Given Zhirinovsky's predilection for behind-the-scenes activities, it may well have appealed to his patriotism to serve the KGB as informant; such a temptation may have been irresistible to him. His participation in a trade delegation to Turkey as long ago as 1969, when he was only 23, is often cited as an indication of long-standing intelligence connections, for such Soviet trade delegations were heavily infiltrated by KGB men and their stooges.

It is the view of Oleg Kalugin, who worked for twenty-five years in KGB intelligence, seven of them in counter-intelligence, that Zhirinovsky was recruited by the KGB. "There is no evidence, but he was obviously infiltrated into the system early on. Look, for instance, at when he was a student and was allowed to travel outside the country freely, even though he was single, with no family. His was the first party to emerge after Communism. He was received by the former KGB chairman, and his party manifestos were printed in the *Pravda* printing house. It is very difficult to get access to it unless you have the support of the Party and its henchmen, the KGB. I believe he has immense support from the old structures." Kalugin recalls seeing Zhirinovsky, as far back as 1990, "roaming the halls of the Kremlin as though he was one of the Party élite. I remember having several conversations with him and thinking he was a borderline psychotic."[2]

Much of his professional life—for example, his time as a trainee in the foreign-broadcast section of the state radio and in the State Committee for Foreign Economic Relations—was spent in jobs that

[2] *The Sunday Times* Magazine, 1 May 1994, p. 27.

would almost certainly have required extensive KGB vetting and monitoring.

After taking evening courses in law at Moscow State University, he finally obtained long-standing employment as a lawyer at the age of 29 in 1975. He worked for Inyurkollegiya, a state-run law firm. One of about fifty lawyers in the concern, he was assigned the task of tracking down Soviet citizens whose relatives in the West had left them alimony, pensions and legacies. He was regarded as well-organized, competent and energetic, becoming the head of the firm's trade union, an important post in a Soviet company.

But his interest in politics led him to make strident pronouncements to the other lawyers in the firm, which made them wary of him. "He would come into my office repeatedly to talk about politics," said Yevgeny Konlichev, his immediate superior at Inyurkollegiya.[3] "He was especially indignant that Russia was surrounded by Turkic people in the south."

At this time, in the early 1980s, the Soviet Union must have seemed politically solid, even if economically stagnant. Anyone ambitious to become a politician would have had to join the Soviet Communist Party. Mr. Konlichev states that Zhirinovsky tried to become a member, even pressing his superiors at the firm to recommend him for Communist Party membership. This Zhirinovsky denies, as he would now do whatever the truth. Mr. Konlichev's account of why the firm refused to do this is as follows: "He was very emotional and gratuitously, not constructively, critical," he says. "His ideas were disorganized, and he insisted fiercely on them," which is true to this day. "His character, the remarks he made, the way he related to people—these did not fit the code of Communist behavior."

Indeed, from this time onwards he tended to vent anti-Communist sentiments; it is, of course, likely that he shared with the Communists

[3] *International Herald Tribune*, 7 March 1994, p. 1.

no beliefs except Soviet nationalism. But rancor at their rejection of him must have fuelled his anti-Communist passion.

In spring 1983 came a rupture with Inyurkollegiya, when he was caught accepting what the firm regarded as improper gifts from a client. Mr. Konlichev says that the rift was brought about by an inheritance case from West Germany. Zhirinovsky's Soviet client had a relative who had died in West Germany and left him, as part of his inheritance, special vouchers permitting him to stay at an exclusive resort. As a sign of his gratitude, the client gave Zhirinovsky the vouchers. According to Konlichev, Zhirinovsky insisted that he had returned the vouchers unused, but Konlichev and other managers in the firm became convinced that he had returned them only after the matter was discovered. "This was the last straw," states Konlichev. It was decided that "unless he wanted more trouble he'd better go."

Zhirinovsky denies that he did anything improper, and, indeed, no charges were brought against him. Konlichev's account of the case may not be the whole truth, since, from Brezhnev's time onwards at least, small-time corruption was endemic; salaries were low; and people supplemented their pay with "gifts" that they expected to get from clients as a matter of course. It is at this time when he was out of work, that, Israeli officials state, he applied for and was sent an invitation to emigrate to Israel. However, the Mir publishing house, an enterprise with more than 600 employees, needed someone with a legal background and offered him a job, so he remained in Russia.

Just as at Inyurkollegiya, he did well at first. But within a year or two his strong political views, in particular his vehement anti-Communism, attracted the attention of the local Communist Party's headquarters. The ideological chief of the Party's branch office contacted the head of Mir, Vladimir Kartsev, urging him to dismiss his wayward employee. Mr. Kartsev, despite being a Communist himself, refused on the grounds that the law did not allow dismissals for political reasons. Again, there is probably more to this than meets the eye. As Mr. Kartsev would well know, dismissals (and rather worse) for political reasons were very common in the Soviet Union.

Zhirinovsky aspired to become the Mir workers' representative, as he had been at Inyurkollegiya. In 1987 he stood as candidate for the council of Moscow's Dzerzhinsky District, named after the first head of CHEKA, the Secret Police in 1917, a forerunner of the KGB. The local Communist Party officials did not welcome his candidacy and rewrote the rules to disqualify him.

These were now the days of *glasnost* and *perestroika*. The struggle against the local Communists was to stand Zhirinovsky in good stead, much as Yeltsin's contest with the Soviet Politburo and Gorbachev did at this very time, when he was mayor of Moscow. Zhirinovsky tried to become one of Mir's fourteen-member employees' council, an innovation of *perestroika*, but was thwarted by Kartsev, who ran a vigorous campaign against him. Zhirinovsky, nevertheless, called his own campaign a "victory," which in a sense it was. For this experience at canvassing helped to develop his oratory and his own brand of demagoguery (which is what politics "is 70 percent about," in his view). He honed the themes that he still exploits today—for instance, better conditions for the workers (in Mir's case, by shifting its line of production from scientific titles to popular books, the higher profits of which would go straight to the firm's employees rather than being invested in the business). He was prefiguring his rhetoric on the electoral stump—where he would promise higher pensions, cheap vodka, a war against crime, the renewal of Russia's military might and his country's resumption of its proper place in the world.

Kartsev then left Mir, and Zhirinovsky made an unsuccessful attempt to replace him as its head. But now he had opening up to him a wider field than the relative backwater of Soviet publishing. The era of *glasnost* was seeing a proliferation of new groups and organizations. From late 1987 Zhirinovsky began to attend as many meetings as he could, so that he could practice his oratory. It was at that time that he joined Shalom, and he explains his participation in the Jewish organization's activities. "What did I want to use

Shalom for?" he told a newspaper correspondent in 1991. "To have a chance to speak." The same is true of his attendance of meetings of the far-right-wing anti-Semitic and ultra-nationalist group, Pamyat, which is closer to his political standpoint.

FROM PRIVATE CITIZEN TO PARTY LEADER

Getting himself known about in this way paid off. The crucial stage of Zhirinovsky's ascent in Russian politics was in the offing. In early 1989 he joined forces with Vladimir Bogachev, a self-styled composer and poet whom he met at a congress of one such organization, the Democratic Union. Bogachev was impressed by his oratory, his legal skills and his linguistic abilities. Bogachev saw him as the figurehead of a new party he was setting up, the Liberal Democratic Party (LDP) of the Soviet Union. At the party's founding congress in March 1990 Zhirinovsky was elected chairman and Bogachev his deputy.

This success, however, proved short-lived. He aroused the mistrust of his colleagues because they suspected that he had links with the Communist regime and the KGB in particular. Seven months later, at the party's second congress in October, it voted for his expulsion.

Zhirinovsky's connections with the Communists in 1990–91 have never been proved and are, of course, strongly denied by him. But not only are ex-party colleagues convinced that they existed, certain Russian politicians, including Gorbachev and Anatoly Sobchak, mayor of St. Petersburg, also think that he was funded and backed by members of the KGB in mid-1990. For he reacted to the reverse of being ejected from the LDP of the Soviet Union by establishing his own party, which he still heads, the Liberal Democratic Party of Russia (LDPR), in the autumn of 1990.

Sobchak's claims to have documentary proof that Gorbachev and others decided at a Politburo meeting in early 1990 to instruct the KGB to set up Zhirinovsky as a stalking horse, a sham "opposition figure," to outflank Yeltsin and give Soviet politics the appearance of multi-party pluralism without disturbing Communist supremacy. The projected upshot was that Zhirinovsky's party would split the democratic vote and scupper Yeltsin.[4]

Gorbachev denies this and suggests that rogue elements in the KGB were responsible. He told a Russian newspaper in January 1992: "Beyond doubt, someone recognized his talents and plans to use them in the future." If Gorbachev puts the matter of his KGB sponsorship "beyond doubt," then it is highly likely to be so, because he is the one man who is in a position to know. All that he is denying is that the person in question was himself.

Vladimir Nazarov, an independent journalist and early biographer of Zhirinovsky, explains who financed the Liberal Democratic Party of Russia in 1990: "In the archives of the Communist Party, deputies found an agreement between the management department of the Central Committee of the Communist Party of the Soviet Union and the company owned by Andrei Zavidiya (who had run for the vice-presidency in the Zhirinovsky election campaign in June 1991). The Bolshevik leaders granted the company an interest-free credit of 3 million roubles . . . Now it is clear who foots the LDPR's bills."[5] Later on the LDPR may well have had to diversify its sources of finance. The big state firms in the military–industrial complex are likely to be one set of backers. Some speculate that Abkhaz drug smugglers are another, in gratitude for LDPR militants' support in the Abkhaz independence movement's war against the Georgians. Abkhazia used to be a province of Georgia and is now of uncertain sovereignty. A third possible source of finance was the East German Communist Party. It is rumored that the East German Communists misappropriated, and then at least partly transferred to Russia, a sum of DM4 million. By early 1991 Zhirinovsky had arrived at center-stage on Russia's political scene, which was threatening to escape its

---

[4] Sobchak is expected to publish a book on the contemporary scene in the summer of 1994.
[5] *New Times International*, October 1992, p. 12.

Soviet management. In the electoral contest for Russia's presidency in June 1991 he won more than 6 million votes, or 8 percent of the total, running third behind Yeltsin and Nikolai Ryzhkev, ex-Soviet premier and Communist candidate. That election assured Yeltsin of his presidential mandate, but the force that could succeed him emerged in the very hour of his electoral triumph, which was to be dramatically confirmed two months later by the failure of the August *coup* plotters and by his own successful defense of the White House (the seat of the Russian Parliament).

A ONE-MAN THINK-TANK

Zhirinovsky's party was from the outset called the Liberal Democratic Party of Russia. Like Yeltsin, he had anticipated the collapse of the Soviet Union and had positioned himself well to shine in its emerging polity. The party has representatives not just in the regions, autonomous republics and military districts of Russia but also in the republics in the Near-Abroad, including in military bases there, where he prides himself on being highly popular. These very representatives stir up trouble with local authorities, which gives Zhirinovsky ideal opportunities to keep himself before the public eye. A firm believer in the dictum that any publicity is good publicity, he wants to remain the most talked-about politician in Russia, to which end his becoming the most notorious politician in the world is a useful adjunct. Hence his flow of wild talk.

He likes holding press conferences at which he expresses indignation at some slight incurred by Russians in the Near-Abroad, whereupon he can give vent to his anger in a torrent of abuse. For instance, when his representative in Estonia, Rozhok, was detained in January 1994, for stirring up inter-ethnic strife, Zhirinovsky said at a press conference, to the cheers of his own militia: **I warn the Estonian government that even if a hair should fall from Rozhok's head, the Estonian government will have to think of the fate of**

900,000 Estonians. I will swap one Rozhok for 900,000 Estonians. If Rozhok is put in an Estonian jail, an end will come to Estonia and Tallinn. We will implement such measures that the Estonians will forget that they are Estonian.

The LDPR has several Cossacks among its backers, especially in the Near-Abroad. General Alexander Lebed, commander of the 14th Army, holds the Cossack Cross for the Defense of Trans-Dnistra, where his army is stationed. He offers strong support to Zhirinovsky, encouraging the Cossacks to do so too. The Cossacks of the Don officially backed Travkin's Democratic Party of Russia, which is largely neo-Fascist, in the December 1993 elections. But with other military and naval commanders expressing support for Zhirinovsky, it may be possible for him to woo the Cossacks away from the electorally far less successful Democratic Party of Russia.

The LDPR has had its share of internal troubles; some deputies have complained about Zhirinovsky's outspoken extremism. Defectors have denounced him as a puppet, installed by reactionary elements in the KGB. "If you want to know about Zhirinovsky," says Leonid Alimov, "just ask Kryuchkev," naming the former KGB chief who was a *coup* plotter in 1991.[6]

In February 1994 a more serious challenge to Zhirinovsky's position was mounted when party treasurer Victor Kobelev defected with Alexander Pronin, another LDPR deputy and shadow minister. They threatened to reveal damaging secrets about Zhirinovsky and the formation of the party. After a brief reunion with Zhirinovsky, Kobelev defected again, threatening to depose Zhirinovsky at the party conference in the first week of April.

In fact, the conference turned out to be a triumph for Zhirinovsky, who was unanimously elected leader for ten years by the 343 delegates, with no new conference to be held until 1997, one year after the next presidential election. Kobelev and other defectors were simply not invited. But, said Kobelev afterwards: "At the moment I am

---

[6] *Time*, 17 February 1992, p. 11.

not using the material [against Zhirinovsky], which I am saving for a serious talk. But if he insults me personally, I will destroy him as a person and as a politician."[7] Two other deputies left in early April, Vladimir Bortyuk and Vladimir Novikov, who respectively headed Oryol and Udmurtia regional branches of the LDPR.

A fifth defector, Anatoly Kashpirovsky, who left at the same time as Kobelev and Pronin, was a great asset to Zhirinovsky in the elections, as he is a well-known hypnotist and faith healer, widely believed to possess occult powers. Until a government ban was imposed, he exercised them on television to mass audiences. He campaigned vigorously for the LDPR in the media in December 1993 and was accused by rival parties of hypnotizing the electorate to vote for Zhirinovsky. Kashpirovsky's defection is certainly a blow but not a fatal one. A strong personality, he is now concentrating on his role as president of the Foundation for Researching the A.M. Kashpirovsky Phenomenon.[8] Zhirinovsky himself has given rise to the "Zhirinovsky phenomenon." A book of that title appeared in Moscow in 1992, a partisan work.[9] Obviously both Zhirinovsky and Kashpirovsky have such massive egos that their coexistence in one party was never likely to last. In what is increasingly becoming a one-man band there is no room for those with independent minds. **The leader and the party are one and the same** (*New York Times*, 5.4.94) is Zhirinovsky's credo.

Kobelev's defection would be more of a nuisance if the material that he has were really damaging. But one reason why he may not have ventilated it already is that it is very likely to implicate him also as a long-time associate and LDPR treasurer. Even if it turns out that Zhirinovsky's KGB connections are proved true, and that dirty money has passed through the party's coffers, this would not nec-

---

[7] *The Times*, 7 April 1994, p. 12.
[8] Directory of Members of the Russian Parliament Elected in December 1993, BBC Monitoring, January 1994, p. 56.
[9] Fenomen Zhirinovskogo, *Kontrolling*, Moscow, 1992.

essarily hurt Zhirinovsky very much in Russia's volatile situation, since the people assume that all politicians are crooked. What they are looking for is a "good" crook or godfather heading a "white mafia" to combat the black mafia that is fleecing the Russian economy. Zhirinovsky has made this very project his number-one priority once he assumes power. He could answer any allegations against him of ill-dealing by claiming to be just such a figure, heading his white mafia to clean up Russia.

A lethal threat to his position, indeed, comes from the mafia, who recognize him as the one politician who might act forcefully against them by using a special police force set up against the mafia in place of an already corrupted police force. Contract killings are now commonplace. One St. Petersburg mafia leader, "Sasha," told a Sunday Times investigator: "Look at Zhirinovsky. If he came to power and started interfering in our business, we would make one phone call to Moscow. That's all. And then no more Zhirinovsky.[10]

Zhirinovsky, however, is well aware of the danger and always goes around with a contingent of his own militia, Zhirinovsky's Falcons, with uniforms and machine-guns. At his weekly public meetings in Moscow and the provinces they flank him on the rostrum and prowl around the generally enthusiastic crowds, keeping an eye open for trouble. A contract taken out on Zhirinovsky would be more difficult to execute than one on other politicians or top bankers, ten of whom were killed in this way in 1993.

An official attempt to prevent Zhirinovsky's rise to power is under way with the help of the Russian Attorney-General's office. This office is considering a request to have Zhirinovsky indicted for violation of Article 71 of the Russian Federation Penal Code, "Propaganda of War." Such a violation is punishable by imprisonment for a term between three and eight years. Zhirinovsky's alleged violation is his calls for a war against Turkey, Iran and Afghanistan in The Last Dash to the South.

[10] The Sunday Times, 7 April 1994, News Review, p. 8.

One reason why Zhirinovsky campaigned successfully for a parliamentary amnesty for Rutskoy, Khasbulatov and the other leaders of the October 1993 *coup* attempt by the previous Russian Parliament is probably that he knew that this would improve his chances of not being indicted himself. If those who actually employ violence against the government and president are let out of jail, how can a politician who simply uses violent language be adjudged sufficiently criminal to be imprisoned? A large fine would not be a serious problem for Zhirinovsky, who always says that anyway the case would be dropped. Something far more decisive than an uncertain legal prosecution would be needed to stop his ascent to supreme power.

HIS THOUGHTS ABOUT HIMSELF, HIS PAST AND HIS FUTURE

I am bad but good for Russia (*Die Zeit*, 14.1.94)

My mother was Russian and my father a lawyer (*New Times International*, February 1992): a classic answer to a question about his ethnic origins. **He was Russian, Wolf Andreyevich Zhirinovsky. My mother called him Volodya** [short for Vladimir] (CSM, 24.12.93). **It would have been easier if she had given me the name Vladimir Vladimirovich, but for bureaucratic reasons or because of the pedantry of the registry, I do not know which, I am called Vladimir Wolfovich. This name is not familiar to Russian ears** (*The Last Dash to the South*). He is clearly uncomfortable with his name.

When a foreign journalist asked him to clarify his racial origins, he replied: **Newspapermen made that up. I never said that my mother was a Russian and my father a lawyer. The simple fact is that I was answering questions at a rally. I read the question: "What nationality was your mother?" I replied: "Russian." A little while later I was handed a piece of paper, and I read: "What was your father's profession?" I replied: "Lawyer." What was I supposed to** do? Just imagine what would have happened if I had got the question about what my father's profession was and I had answered: "Russian." They would have called me a lunatic. Zhirinovsky went on to outline his genealogy, all the way back to his great-grandfathers and great-grandmothers. All of them were pure Russians, no mixtures. Granted, my father's parents were from Poland, but Poland isn't a state really. It's a Russian province (*Current Digest of the Post-Soviet Press*, 12.1.94).

I've had thousands of blood tests. If you have specialists who could find at least 5 percent Jewish blood in me, I would be proud. But there is none. (CSM, 24.12.93).

Zhirinovsky is the common man personified. I myself am an ordinary citizen. I represent the middle stratum which earns two hundred roubles and lives in a two-room apartment. I am just like you, and I understand that these awful prices in commercial and cooperative stores are beyond our pockets . . . Women of Russia . . . I know things have been hard for you . . . A few days before [my mother] died she said: "Volodya, there is nothing to remember." In all her seventy-three years she had not known a single day of joy . . . I share all of your anxieties: the eternal lines, the shortages . . . constant worry about how to feed the family properly . . . You must be provided for. (Moscow Radio, 11.6.91)

I was born among Russians, so I consider myself to have been born in Russia itself. (*Financial Times*, 9.12.93)

It was a joyless childhood. All eighteen years . . . Even my bed was not my own. I slept on a trunk . . . Mum never had any time. She was working . . . Sometimes I would not see her for days on end (*The Last Dash to the South*). I had no place to play. My clothes were bought at the market, the clothes of dead people (*La Stampa*, 16.12.93). I was always hungry. I was fed from the cafeteria in which my mother worked. The food was awful and, of course, it caused gastritis. In the flat there were no children's books, no toys, no papers, no telephone (*Die Zeit*, 14.1.94). Life forced me to suffer from the very day, the moment, the instant, of my birth. Society could give me nothing. (*Time*, 27.12.93)

In his description of suffering and joylessness he falls back upon another commonplace topic: suffering as preparation for great achievement. A painter or a composer may need the experience of misfortune to be able to create. It was the same with me. Being isolated by loneliness . . . has served the purpose of enabling me to understand better, and more profoundly, the political process. The constant feeling of not being satisfied has stimulated me. (*Die Zeit*, 14.1.94)

His descriptions of his deprivations in the emotional and social desert of his early life may be heartfelt at least sometimes, but they may equally well be intended to conjure up in the minds of his audience and readers biblical images of prophets girding their loins in preparation for their mission, especially since he goes on describing the vague intimations of a barefooted youngster: I was not able to comprehend it then, but I felt instinctively that I was destined for a great role in politics. (*Die Zeit*, 14.1.94)

I remember in school that one girl had a ball-point pen and I didn't. Or I would visit a home where they had hot water, but we didn't. If I had lived in good conditions, warm and well-fed, maybe I wouldn't have become involved in politics. (*Wall Street Journal Europe*, 14.12.93, quoted from *The Last Dash to the South*)

Even in early childhood something dawned on me. It was a kind of ultimate idea that was like the intellect governing the world. Even when I was a small boy walking along the quiet street from home towards the Nikolskaya church and the Nikolsky market, there was something . . . thoughts of something great were hovering in my head . . . And this came to pass. This was no accident . . . An educated man with two university degrees who speaks European languages; where did he pop up from, this throwback to the prosperous Russia of the last century? (*The Last Dash to the South*)

Try to find another country that is being destroyed and plundered as systematically as Russia. I am not simplifying the matter. Each decision is a hard one. It's just that I'm an expert in what I am doing; I provide prompt answers to questions because I have them. I have been thinking about them for thirty years.

Why do you ignore the fact that Zhirinovsky graduated from Moscow University with honors, that he speaks four languages and has traveled extensively throughout Russia and the world? Hence my prompt solutions. (*Izvestiya*, 30.1.93)

Ideology won't get in my way! I am free of dogma. My political views have always been the same as they are now. I come from a long line of lawyers. My grandfather was a lawyer under the tsar. My father was a lawyer—before the war, under the Stalin regime. I am a lawyer, and my son is studying law. So that is one point. Throughout the world, 80 percent of leaders are arts graduates. I have a double arts background. (Soviet Television, 22.5.91)

An American offered me $10 million to leave politics. I told him: "Never." I steer the boat here. I know the course. No one else knows. (*Die Zeit*, 4.2.94)

I was born in 1946, the year of the dog. Dogs are faithful, sincere and always at your service. My party will never betray our voters. (*Economist*, 18.12.93)

I have never been a Communist. Neither I nor our party has ever given any support to the present political regime. This is a 100-percent guarantee that we are different. (Mayak Radio, Moscow, 8.12.93)

I have never read *Mein Kampf.* (*Die Zeit*, 14.1.94)

I am not a Fascist. On the contrary, I have always made efforts in the struggle for human rights. (ITAR–TASS, 13.12.93)

He prides himself on being an expert in geography, which, as he put it, is his favorite occupation. He once gave the former French diplomat Rolf Gauffin a map with the new frontiers of Central and Eastern Europe drawn on it. He signed it—just as Stalin signed the map showing the partition of Poland in the German-Soviet pact of 1939.

Asked about his connection with the former KGB, he gave the categorical assurance: I have no connections with the former or the present KGB. I would gladly have had connections with the KGB, as it was the most powerful political police in the world. Had I been connected with the KGB, I would be sitting in the Kremlin now and not in this small town on the shore of a lake (Quoted by Radio Slovenia, Ljubljana, 28.1.94). On an another occasion, when asked the same question, he replied: I never worked for the KGB. I might have gone further if I had. (*The Times*, 21.12.93)

I represent the party that won Russia's first free elections. Our party came first. The Russian people elected this party knowing that it was the party of a new Russia, the party of a new foreign policy, the party of cooperation with the Serb people. (A speech in Bjeljina reported by Tanjug, Belgrade, 31.1.94)

Zhirinovsky is a real populist. He is willing to incur the wrath of politicians with pronouncements like: I have no wish to be of service to any politician. He points out that he always has the little man in mind.

Thousands of people have kissed my hands. (*La Stampa*, 16.12.93)

The leader and the party are one and the same. (*The New York Times*, 5.4.94)

I have never allowed myself a single extremist escapade in my life. (*Time*, 27.12.93)

There is no doubt that I'll be president of Russia because there are no other candidates. If elections are held this year, I'll get 55 percent of the vote; if they are held in two years' time it will be even better because then I'll be 50, and the people will give me 70 percent of the vote as a present . . . There are no other candidates because all politicians who are in any way connected with those in power are responsible for poverty, inflation and organized crime . . . Polls which say that I have only 6 percent support for the presidency are silly nonsense; they also said that I would not get into Parliament. The press only publishes these figures because of the mafia, which wants to liquidate me and pays the papers to sully my reputation . . . As soon as I get into the Kremlin I'll order the liquidation of organized crime—10,000 *mafiosi* will be arrested and publicly executed . . . When I go the Russian provinces, people kiss my hands and throw themselves upon me to embrace me, for they know that I am the only one to stand up for the rights of the people—no one believes the slanders that you journalists publish, such as that I'm a Fascist, an anti-Semite and so on. (*Yediot Akhronot*, 16.3.94)

I am moderate in all things. (*Time*, 27.12.93)

Zhirinovsky concedes that he has a weakness: **My only vice is a weakness for frontier posts, for their being in place. If some unclean force moved them inside Russia, Zhirinovsky's party would return them to their place, but within the framework of the law.** (ITAR–TASS report, Moscow World Service Radio, 2.4.94)

REFLECTIONS ON RACE AND NATIONALISM

Nationalism? It's a disease just like Fascism. We'll get rid of it in the third millennium. (*La Stampa*, 16.12.93)

Apparently we must deal with minorities as America did with the Indians and Germany with the Jews. (*Time*, 27.12.93)

There is another important aspect of Zhirinovsky's ideology—his stance against any form of what he calls "internationalism," political, economic or social. The internationalist approach of the former Soviet government is what he mainly objects to. **The idea of internationalism has been spreading around the world for a century and a half. With the growth of capital, frontiers became weaker and weaker. Improvements in the means of transport and of communications have made the task of industrialists increasingly easier, the industrialists of all countries united. The "specter of Communism" appeared in response to that: the idea of a united proletariat haunted Europe; and this fraternity, like the fraternity of the Rothchilds and the Rockefellers, has remained alive and influential to this day through the force of its spirit and its ideology** (*Le Monde*, 23.12.93).

He sees the history of Russia from 1917 onwards as a series of alternations between national and international policies, one or the other gaining the upper hand under successive leaders. [Lenin] **put the internationalist interests of the working class above national interests. But world revolution never took place. However, the rea-**

son for that was not, as some scholars would have us believe, because the idea was senseless. Had Trotsky been the leader, the idea would have been realized. The enormous potential of a gigantic country, its powerful army and the influence of the Komintern would have yielded results. But power in the USSR was seized by a "Caucasian group," which had little connection with the Komintern . . . Stalin tended to limit the activities of the Komintern, turning toward isolation from Europe, both from the Communist and from the capitalist part of it. (*Le Monde*, 23.12.93)

We should think about saving the white race because today the white race is a minority in the world. It is a minority that needs to be protected and saved. If we don't fight against this danger—the Islamic danger, the Asian danger—then in the future we will have a religious danger and, finally, religious wars where we will all be swamped by what is called the Yellow Peril. (*Time*, 27.12.1993)

The notion behind internationalism is that of mixture; nationalism comprises the notion of quality. Nationalism is like a self-contained flat and not a communal boarding house . . . If we acknowledge that we are constructing a national state, with a national ideology and without any kind of "Eurasianism" or "Atlantism," then our first task is to establish national frontiers. They must be clearly defined and then locked tight (*Le Monde*, 23.12.93). The "Eurasianism" to which Zhirinovsky refers here was originally a movement of Russian émigrés in the 1920s who thought that, for Russia, Asia would be more important than the West. It was one of the many anti-Western tendencies in Russia, and at the time of the collapse of the Soviet Union it was revived for that very reason. "Atlantism" is the enemy of the "Eurasianists"; it proposes an Atlantic empire of the USA and international Zionism, whose nefarious influence and aggressive hostility—so the theory goes—can be repelled only by the bastion of Eurasia, led, of course, by Russia with its old Soviet borders.

National socialism unites the most important principles of socialism with national ideas. National socialism has nothing in common with Hitlerism. Hitler has discredited national socialism. In addition, in elaborating his doctrines he borrowed the idea of . . . world revolution. Only a very tenuous line separates the idea of wanting a world revolution from striving for world domination. National socialists do not need to dominate the world . . .

The philosophy of a national socialist is that of the common man, of the *petit bourgeois,* if you will, who wants a quiet life in his own apartment, a wife who loves him, healthy children, a secure job; on Sundays he wants to go out into his garden or to the country; and he wants a holiday once a year. He does not wish to bother anybody, but he does not wish to be bothered either. He is not a hero—not at all.

He does not long to plough the frozen earth with his tank in the name of who knows what ideal. A beggar causes him distaste, and he feels some resentment of the very rich. He wants to be sure that his daughter will not be raped in the street at night and that his son's head will not be bashed in with a bottle. He is absolutely not fanatical; unlike Hitler, he needs no cult or occultism. But he wants to be able to look up to his leaders and feel that, because of their intelligence, they deserve the position they have. (*Le Monde,* 23.12.93)

Division along ethnic lines brings about civil war, dredges up the complication and inexorability of the nationalities issue, which is the most intractable of issues and has not yet been resolved anywhere in the world—not in affluent Canada, in cultured France or in formerly fraternal Yugoslavia. Everywhere it takes on a bloody aspect. (Soviet Television, 22.5.91)

Our most vexed issue is the nationalities question. I graduated with distinction from the institute of the countries of Asia and

Africa. My profession has a link with the inhabitants of the majority of Turkic-speaking regions—Kazakhstan, Central Asia, the Transcaucasus and the Near East. I could address the Turkic-speaking deputies in their own language at this very moment.

It would be nice for them if the president of Russia understood them and knew the culture and language of this multi-million-strong people of our country, of our Russia. So that they can understand me, I'll switch languages. [Continuing in Turkish] Today we may elect the president, but what sort of president he will be will depend upon you. [Resuming in Russian] I'll revert to Russian because I have great respect for it and I'd very much like the whole country to respect the Russian language, just as it is respected today in Europe and America, whereas in the Baltic and some other regions they have a very negative attitude toward it. (Soviet Television, 22.5.91)

There is no reason to fear Islamic fundamentalism. Islamic fundamentalism is the establishment of an order, of traditions that characterize peoples in the south: polygamy, respect for the old, submission, traditional crafts, the Koran. In what way is that bad for us Russians? (*Le Monde*, 23.12.93)

Fundamentalism is nationalism. (*Le Monde*, 23.12.93)

It is, in general, a question of saving the white race from a threat to its existence. The whites constitute 8 percent of the total today. Do you think that 92 percent will put up for very long with 8 percent living in better regions, enjoying better diets and longer life expectancy? This 92 percent will claim its rights yet. (*New Times International*, October 1992)

Blacks? America will ask us for help to put a stop to the propagation of colored people. (*La Stampa*, 16.12.1993)

Russia is threatened by Islam and non-Russian ethnic groups. The Turks are taking over too much power in Germany and the Arabs in France, and blacks may soon take over white cities in America. Whites would be very upset in that case, and that is what is happening in Russia (AP, 15.3.94).

In reply to a question as to whether he was racist on top of everything else, Zhirinovsky said: Not at all. Why do you think so? I am talking about the threat to the white nation. If a robber intends to break into my house, do I violate his rights to rob my house if I try to stop him?

I am against . . . Zionists. Why am I anti-Zionist? Because of the October Revolution, of course. And because of the thirty Zionists in Parliament; one of them is actually called Sabbath. This Mr. Sabbath is particularly bad. Why are Zionists so bad? Because they make Russia weak. They do that because they want to emigrate to Israel. But they should rather stay here. It is, in fact, easier for a state when there is only one nationality. Russia is, however, multinational and should stay so (*Die Zeit*, 4.3.94). Zhirinovsky uses the word "Zionist" in the sense in which it was used in the USSR, where anti-Semitism was officially unacceptable, illegal. It is a widely held view that Communism in Russia was a Jewish plot.

Although we are not anti-Semitic, we won't tolerate an increase in the strength of the Jews. (*Financial Times*, 14.12.93)

People who call themselves Jews are provoking a wave of anti-Semitism . . . To avoid anti-Semitism, we should increase the number of Russian faces on TV. (*Observer*, 19.12.93)

On Russian television there should be pretty girls with blond hair and blue eyes, women who speak good Russian . . . Gaidar is half-Jewish, and the IMF forms part of an international Jewish conspiracy. (*Frankfurter Allgemeine*, 16.12.93)

About the Jews: **You are the richest people on earth; I envy you.**
(*La Stampa*, 16.12.93)

**I will never agree with a situation in which 2 million Russian Jews
rule a country where another 150 million Russians simply have to
obey them.** (*Time*, 27.12.93)

GEOPOLITICS

With a consummate demagogue like Zhirinovsky it is not always
easy to know which of his ideas are meant simply to find favor with
his immediate audience and which should be seen as having a more
general relevance to his policies. In any case, during his tour in the
former Yugoslavia at the end of January 1994 he addressed two
audiences: those present, or listening to broadcasts, and the audience
back home, especially the Russian leadership.

Both Kozyrev, the Russian Foreign Minister, and his deputy, Vi-
taly Churkin, made statements that gave the impression that they
were trying to catch up with Zhirinovsky. Andrey Kozyrev, however,
took the trouble to deny this. In a statement made on 10 March
1994 he said that Russia foreign policy was not being formulated
under pressure from Zhirinovsky. "If we had not been accused of
acting on Zhirinovsky's orders, we would have talked even tougher,"
said Kozyrev.

Considering that the Russians have never managed to penetrate
so far into the Balkans, we can only wonder what else Kozyrev hoped
to achieve by tough talk. The Serbs must have been impressed by
the promptness with which Zhirinovsky's promises were translated
into action: Russian troops arrived in Bosnia, proving that the great
Russian nation is, indeed, behind the Serbs. Marshal Tito, who
resolutely opposed letting Russians into Yugoslavia for decades, must
be turning in his grave.

In foreign policy we must move from an east–west relationship to a north–south relationship . . . We will come to an accommodation with Germany. A strong Turkey and Iran are in the south, but Russian soldiers will no longer shed their blood in the Transcaucasus. We will reach accord with the Turks and with Iran. (Speech to the Russian Congress of People's Deputies, Russian TV, 22.5.91)

According to Zhirinovsky, Russia is losing its position in the Middle East, where Iraq is its most reliable ally. To the east and south Russia ought to bank on building allied relationships with Japan, China and India. As for the allied relationship with India, it will depend largely on whether Russia helps it to repel the Muslim threat. In Zhirinovsky's view, access to the Indian Ocean should become a goal of Russia's foreign policy to the south. In this case Afghanistan, Iran and Turkey will have to be "neutralized," which, according to him, will be applauded in Europe. (Zhirinovsky's statement to the press, INTERFAX, 24.11.92)

All we want is three countries: Afghanistan, Iran and Turkey. Russia can play an historic role in saving the world from the spread of Islam, from the spread of international terrorism. (*Time*, 27.12.93)

I had already begun to develop my own geopolitical concept . . . The last "dash to the south" and to Russian outlets on the shores of the Indian Ocean and the Mediterranean Sea is really a measure designed to save the Russian nation. For when other parties talk of cutting off Kazakhstan, Kirghizia and Central Asia, they do not realize that we are pushing Russia into the tundra, where mineral resources are all that can exist, where nothing can live and develop . . . The development of civilization has always begun in the south. We may quite unnecessarily drive ourselves into barren regions and destroy the nation once and for all . . . So the idea emerged of the last dash—last because it will probably be the last repartition of the world and must be carried out suddenly, swiftly and effectively. This will immediately solve all our problems, because we will gain tranquility. We will also gain tranquil neighbors. Friendly India. Enmity will cease for ever. (*The Last Dash to the South*)

The future prospect which I envision is the gradual abandonment of the national-territorial division, which will help us to solve the nationality issue . . . Order needs to be restored. (Zhirinovsky's campaign statement, TRUD, 11.6.91)

For North America there will be Latin America; for Western Europe there will be Africa; for China and Japan, there will be South-East Asia . . . For Russia there will be only three states: Turkey, Iran, Afghanistan. It is a region of vitally important interests for Russia . . . And further to the south the warm Indian Ocean . . . If we unite the Russian north [with its heavy industry] with the south, where there are basic foodstuffs and raw materials for light industry, then, *yes*, we will have our market economy. (Zhirinovsky's article published in the LDPR newspaper, *Liberal*, No. 2, 1993)

One day Greater Germany, a new Russia and India will form a new *entente*. Then there will be no problems in the world. India and Russia will neutralize China; Russia and Germany can control Europe; and Russia and the Balkan states will solve all problems in the Balkans. (*Die Welt*, 29.1.94)

Zhirinovsky promises that if he comes to power, he will restore order in Europe by forming an alliance with Germany. **Let the Germans move east to the Soviet–German border while we move south.** He has also expressed his support for the liberation struggle of the Kurds with the help of **Cuban mercenaries and Russian weapons.** (Zhirinovsky's stump speech, INTERFAX, 7.5.92)

GENERAL VIEWS ABOUT THE WORLD

Fascism: A terrible disease that we have got rid of. (*La Stampa*, 16.12.93)

I am not a Fascist. On the contrary. I have always made efforts in the struggle for human rights. (ITAR-TASS, 13.12.93)

You are not a genuine Fascist [he said to Alexander Nevsorov]. You only want a civil war because, as a journalist, you want something to write about. You're not really brown like me. You're reddish-brown. (*Die Zeit*, 4.3.94)

During his visit to Slovenia he expressed his disapproval of the disintegration of the Slavic states into a host of "statelets," adding that if this trend continues the entire world will break up because the readjustment of borders in one case will encourage the same practice in another. (Quoted on Radio Slovenia, Ljubljana, 28.1.94)

His reply to the question of which historical figures he most admires was: For Russia, General Kutuzov; for France, De Gaulle; for Germany, Roosevelt. When one of his aides pointed out that Roosevelt was American, he added with perfect unconcern: Well, all right, Frederick the Great for Germany. (*The Times*, 21.12.93)

That's all that politics is about—demagoguery. Politics is 70 percent lies and terror. Without lies and terror, you can't do politics . . . But I personally always tell the truth. (*Time*, 27.12.93)

The commonest major blunder, and Russia's mishap, was that they gave us gifts for what should have been sold for money. Now we have modern arms, which cost more than 30 billion roubles, but we are not selling them. We have quit the market.

For instance, the Volga–Urals military district had 24,000 idle tanks. India wanted them, but we did not sell them to India, preferring to scrap them instead. That is what I am trying to draw attention to—the demolition of arms for which certain countries are prepared to pay hard currency. Saddam Hussein is now prepared to pay us $10 billion, Iraq's debt to Russia, but for the past two years no Russian leader has met him, no diplomat, no journalist. Except myself. What Hussein said to me was, "Russian diplomacy is amazing." I told them, "Take this money, it's yours," but they wouldn't take it . . . Why should we inflict suffering on ourselves? Let's make others suffer. (*Izvestiya*, 30.11.93)

THE WEST, ITS VALUES AND ITS PRACTICES

In a TASS report (World Service in English, 18.12.91) Zhirinovsky claimed that the CIA is in the process of waging a weaponless "third world war" against Russia. Instead of sending the technology Russia needs to overcome its current economic crisis, the USA is trying to poison the Russian people with **vodka, Pepsi and propaganda.**

INTERFAX, commenting on Zhirinovsky's speech (7.5.92), quoted him as saying that the West, after robbing Africa and Latin America, has now started robbing Russia. He also claimed that the West is supported by Democratic Russia and the government, who are **fulfilling Western orders and embezzling, not so much because** of a tendency toward corruption, but because they realize that they will not remain in power long.

The world should think twice before opposing us—after all, is it really desirable to have a third world war? (*Financial Times*, 14.12.93)

During his tour of the Balkans at the end of January 1994, Zhirinovsky found a good opportunity to air his anti-Western views. In a speech in Bijelijna he spoke of "some foreign countries"—an expression reminiscent of old Soviet-style speeches—in a clear reference to the NATO decision to bomb Serbian artillery positions around Sarajevo if they were not withdrawn by the deadline stated in the ultimatum.

They have two standards of democracy. The destruction of the Serbs and the Russians is, according to them, democracy, but when we are defending ourselves they call it Fascism. We are not going to fall for these double standards. I therefore wish the Serbs to become even stronger. I wish you courage, strength and optimism. Look ahead proudly, as a great nation. The great Russian nation is behind you. (Bosnian Serb Radio First Program, reported by Tanjug, Belgrade, 30.1.94).

The Anti-Russian conspiracy of the West is an age-old theme in Russian political rhetoric. In Soviet days the talk was of the anti-socialist, reactionary machinations of the imperialists; now, following much the same line but without the ideological coloring, we hear of cunning Westerners going to Russia, exploiting it and creating a havoc. Before the December 1993 elections, Zhirinovsky accused the (Russian) producers of a film about himself: The film was intended to scare people, and I think it was paid for by Western services (Independent, 10.12.93). In the film there was a picture of Zhirinovsky with the caption: "I am the Almighty! I am a tyrant! I shall follow in Hitler's footsteps."

Yours is a democracy that will not succeed. You won't intimidate me. You are all losers, he said in Strasbourg. He was furious because the French authorities did not let him go anywhere else in France . . . We are ahead of you. Russia has more rights and liberties than you have in Europe . . . You [the Council of Europe] have members who use their armed forces to fight against democracy. He was referring to Turkey and Britain. He also accused the

West of **contaminating** Russia **with the Communist virus.** (Reuter, 12.4.94)

THOUGHTS ON WAR (NUCLEAR AND CONVENTIONAL) AND PEACE

Zhirinovsky has always favored peace, as he affirmed on Radio Slovenia (28.1.94). **We are for disarmament. Russia will destroy its nuclear weapons**—after everybody else. (*La Stampa*, 16.12.93).

The twenty-first century will be **our century,** he predicts. **We are washing away these scabs, this dirt that has accumulated over the whole twentieth century. Sometimes this causes blood. This is bad.** But blood, he adds in a final gruesome flourish, **may be necessary in order finally to wash away this contagion that was introduced into the center of Russia from the West to poison the country and undermine it from within**—**through Communism, nationalism, cosmopolitanism, through the influence of alien religions, alien ideas, an alien way of life. We will put an end to this.** (*New Republic*, 14.2.94)

Who Is This Man Anyway?

There is one thing everybody agrees on: Zhirinovsky is a great talker. He smothers his audience with torrents of words and cascades of banalities seasoned with dreams and threats. He is charismatic in so far as he can hold an audience and can handle his television programs with exceptional skill; apart from that, what has he to offer, if that is the right word? What is he, people ask: a state-of-the-art Hitler or just a clown? Underneath all the nonsense, what is his actual stance: a back-to-basics "petit-bourgeoisism," or does he aspire to be a nuclear Robin Hood? Is he an unscrupulous and cynical opportunist, who will accept a bribe, when all is said and done, or is he a stalwart, though misguided, Russian patriot? Since he wants to be all things to all men, he may be all of these or none. Kurt Tucholsky, a noted figure on the German literary scene, said about Hitler before 1933: "The man is simply not there—he's just the clamor he provokes" (*Die Zeit*, 14.1.94). Should Zhirinovsky come to power, would his actions be as aggressive as his words are now, or will the words do the job of actions?

If you try to make sense of his stated plans, you do not find a coherent policy. His economic policy is to sell lots and lots of arms to more and more people, and there are subjects upon which, in the midst of a sea of words, he hardly touches. Could it be that he has a subtext, a hidden agenda, about which he talks only with his powerful backers (if any), a hidden game plan that, if laid over what he actually says, would reveal the "figure in the carpet"? But, before we discuss that, let us see who is most apprehensive about Zhirinovsky's unexpected rise, and what they have done about foiling his scheme.

THE BLACK RAINBOW OF RUSSIAN HOPES

In the lands of the former Soviet Union there are two main groups that fear his ascent to power: his opponents in Russian political life, and most people in the former republics, now independent states, since his declared ambition is for Russia to repossess them.

Who would welcome his coming to power? First of all, his followers, who voted for his party in the December 1993 elections and, secondly, such backers as he may have—that is, backers who have at their disposal political or other means with which to promote him. This is one subject that Zhirinovsky does not talk about. He has distanced himself from the KGB and from any part of the Soviet power structure, but can we be sure that at least one section of the KGB does not support him? There have been suggestions that the KGB, recognizing his political talents, set his party up as a token opposition party when the Soviet Union was still in place, and then, seeing his erratic ways, threw him over. He has always strongly denied any links with the KGB, which he would do both if there were some or not. Perhaps he is still supported by these hidden backers with considerable influence and means at their disposal to help him establish countrywide organizations and even, as some people now suggest, rig the results of the December elections in his favor more successfully than other parties were able to do. Would they have provided him with the necessary funds for running a countrywide organization indispensable for rigging millions of votes?

As for other backers, this time abroad, who may have helped him financially? Saddam Hussein springs to mind; Zhirinovsky has always emphasized his friendship with the Iraqi leader, but he usually confines himself to generalities (helping him in his struggle against the West, sympathizing with his aim to reoccupy Kuwait, which, he says, has the same status for Iraq as Crimea has for the Russians).

The help of European extreme-right groups has also been suggested, but that could not be very substantial. Former German Communist Party funds are also mentioned. Or is it possible that he is backed by one or more mafia organizations inside Russia, despite his protestations against the mafia and gangsterism, the elimination of which is at the top of his agenda after coming to power? Or could there be a group of foreign *mafiosi* who hope to gain influence through the future president of Russia?

What has the West done so far to throw a spanner in his works apart from calling him a grotesque clown? Zhirinovsky's main propaganda complaint against the West is that, far from helping Russia, it wants to ruin it and make it serve Western interests.

True, the West has not done much in the economic sphere, and very little in the way of any other kind of real assistance. In days gone by Germany gave DM80 billion (about US $50 billion) to the Soviet Union, but that did not save either the Soviet economy or Gorbachev.

Then the new Russian government, after the collapse of the Soviet Union, embraced a plan for Western-type reforms that Gorbachev had shelved. That raised new hopes that things would improve. But so far reforms have not done anything to alleviate the crisis, and consequently the reformers' position has been considerably weakened. There had been some financial aid, a billion dollars here and there, some of which has probably ended up, through mafia pockets, in Western banks. Are those IMF and World Bank plans and schemes quite wrong? After all, no one has ever had the experience of making a capitalist giant out of a Communist superpower. It may be an impossible task, certainly if it is done simultaneously with changing a totalitarian political system into a democratic multi-party one.

The reformers have started backtracking, and Zhirinovsky can declare with satisfaction that they have heeded his advice. It does not look as if the West is going to do anything spectacular in the field of financial or economic aid to Russia. The standing of the West in the eyes of the Russian people has fallen considerably. They feel that it has deceived them by omission. The Western media have commented at length about the advantages of market economy and the excellence of democracy but have said little about the problems of transition. Anti-Western attitudes are gaining ground, and anti-Western organizations are mushrooming. So far so good, thinks Zhirinovsky.

LET'S GIVE HIM A LEG-UP!

Far from thwarting Zhirinovsky's schemes, the West has started putting one into practice. Zhirinovsky, in an interview given to *Krasnaya Zvezda* in May 1991, outlined a scheme according to which Russian soldiers under contract for hard currency could perform tasks assigned by the world community. He suggested such a peacekeeping role in other contexts, for the countries south of Russia; that is one of the plans outlined in his book, *The Last Dash to the South*. So Western reluctance to get involved on the ground in Bosnia gave an opportunity to the Russians to penetrate the Balkans as a peacekeeping force (with the enthusiastic support of the local Serbs, of course), and they hope that their "Orthodox/Slavic Brotherhood" with the Serbs will enable them to gain a firm foothold in the Balkans, which has been a Russian ambition for a long time (Tito's careful policies, to Stalin's fury, foiled that plan in the 1940s and 1950s). So, is Zhirinovsky's plan, including the hope of gaining access to the Mediterranean through Montenegro, for instance, in the process of re-alization?

What about the subjects on which Zhirinovsky is generally silent? We cannot tell whether his nuclear threats are just verbal flourishes, nor how he is going to make use of Russia's military and, especially, nuclear capacity.

FLYING KITES

What can his repeated recourse to the idea of unleashing a third world war mean? Sometimes he seems to be on the point of making it clear. On other occasions he appears to be flying kites.

In an interview that he gave to Alexander Yanov, which appeared in the *New Times International* in October 1992, we read that he said the following in reply to the question of how he was going to fulfill his promise to feed the Russian nation in seventy-two hours: "It is very simple really; I shall order 1.5 million troops into the former GDR, brandish arms there, nuclear arms included and there'll be enough food to go round."

Yanov, to whom he appears to say things that he does not mention so frankly elsewhere, in his article in the *Los Angeles Times*, 4 March 1994, writes the following: "Zhirinovsky does not believe that the current Russian crisis can be resolved in the domestic area. Like Hitler, he sees the "salvation of the nation" in war and conquest. But not in a nuclear war, and not in one with either the West or with China. His quarrel is with the Muslim world (the only exception being his current friend, ally and financier, Saddam Hussein). Its riches, and especially its oil, he promises, would save Russia. He recognizes that "some people" in Teheran, Ankara or Riyadh may object to their countries becoming Russian provinces, **but the whole world should think that if Russia needs it . . . it is for the best.** Besides, **the majority of mankind is interested in dissecting the**

Muslim world. **The Muslim peril has to be eliminated.** This would supposedly be Russia's greatest service to modern civilization.

But that is not all, although, as Yanov notes, this is Zhirinovsky's *Mein Kampf* in briefest outline. "What does Zhirinovsky think the rest of the world would do while his armies marched to the oil fields of the Middle East in order to monopolize this vital strategic resource? Zhirinovsky has a quite impressive answer to this. According to him, the rest of the world would do precisely what it did when Hitler's armies marched around Europe—nothing. This is what Russia's "nuclear shield" is all about: to ensure a new Munich on the part of the West. And, indeed, would any Western government risk annihilation for the sake of Turkey, let alone Iran?

Richard W. Judy, writing in the *National Review* (21.3.94), says: "Zhirinovsky carries a big stick. If the European, Asian and American great powers refuse to acquiesce in Russia's "Last Dash to the South" he will be prepared "to make life very unpleasant." He has never stated precisely what unpleasant measures he might take, but his remarks imply clearly that he means "nuclear blackmail, abrogation of arms-control agreements and other militarily hostile measures."

There we have a plan hinted at strongly by Zhirinovsky. First of all, like a "nuclear Robin Hood" (Yanov's words) he can blackmail the West with nuclear weapons to provide food and, presumably, other kinds of help. The threat of a nuclear strike could also be used in the Middle East. Let us take one scenario. In agreement with Saddam Hussein, he would send Russian armies against Iran (having first made sure that Azerbaijan was under control—he is more than halfway there with the flexible former Communist Party chief, Aliyev, in the presidential seat). He would attack Iran from the north, while Saddam Hussein would attack from the west. They would probably succeed in subduing Iranian resistance and set up a Quisling government with the help of Iranian opposition to the *mullahs*, either in Iran, or abroad, or both. At that point he would go no further. The two aggressors would divide the oil loot; at the same time an independent (independent in the sense that Kazakhstan and the Baltic states were independent in Stalin's time) Kurdish state would be set up to spite the Turks. He would not attack Turkey, he would only supply arms, money, etc., to Kurdish rebels in Turkey. Would the West risk a nuclear war in defense of Iran? Probably not. Would it risk a nuclear war to defend the Turkish stand against the Turks? That would not be a very attractive proposition either. Russia and Iraq could stop at that point and let the West get used to the *status quo*.

But what about his other plans, the incorporation of the Baltic states, Finland, Poland? In exchange for a "free hand from Karachi to Constantinople," Zhirinovsky might be prepared to give up Russia's historically justified claims. In the east he would abandon its claim to the return of Alaska and cede ownership of the Kuril Islands to Japan. Then again, he could occupy the Baltic states or any other state outside NATO and threaten a nuclear attack if anyone showed any inclination to stop him. Would the West risk a nuclear war to save Romania, Slovakia or Hungary?

The West would probably rather let him get on with these plans so long as he did not go further. Could he not learn from Hitler's mistakes, stop after the first round and give the world a breathing space? But if the West does not acquiesce, what then? Here we have to go back to what Mao Tse-Tung said to the Finnish ambassador in 1955, quoted in the Preface.

The next, possibly better, scenario: Zhirinovsky takes power. He does not go beyond a big push against the Russian mafia—at least those parts of it that are not his allies—but through a dictatorship, settles down to establish his version of national socialism (see Chapter 6), his own version of "back to basics," to satisfy the aspirations of the "little man" or, rather, to give the impression of doing so. By the time people realize that what they expected is not happening, they will be in no position to object: the dictatorship he keeps promising will be firmly in place, with some political "liberties" perhaps— by comparison with the Stalin era, no racial persecutions except for a new, strict *propiska* system preventing Central Asians and Caucasians from coming to Russia proper (his "Berlin Wall" along the north of the Caucasus), a Potemkin multi-party system, Potemkin elections of the Soviet era, etc. And then he will turn round and say: "We have established Fascism with a human face," and everybody will heave a sigh of relief.

What if Zhirinovsky were shot or otherwise eliminated from the race? Is it likely that in a ruined Russia, whose only strength is military, somebody else would take a leaf out of Zhirinovsky's book and implement some of his "milder" policies? Vladimir Nazarov, Zhirinovsky's first independent biographer, said in 1992: "Even if Zhirinovsky himself disappears from the CIS's turbulent political scene tomorrow, the 'Zhirinovsky phenomenon' will not. He may well be replaced by someone else, someone more intelligent, better-mannered, more restrained—and of Russian nationality."

Russia is not likely to resolve ingrained national problems without a major disaster, and we should wonder who else will be dragged into it. On the other hand, it may be that Zhirinovsky, or someone more or less like him, is simply a tool, the "hidden hand" of the Russian soul yearning for self-purification through the ultimate catastrophe, "the figure in the carpet."

So what is the point of asking whether Zhirinovsky is like Hitler?

FOR THE BEST IN PAPERBACKS, LOOK FOR THE

In every corner of the world, on every subject under the sun, Penguin represents quality and variety—the very best in publishing today.

For complete information about books available from Penguin—including Pelicans, Puffins, Peregrines, and Penguin Classics—and how to order them, write to us at the appropriate address below. Please note that for copyright reasons the selection of books varies from country to country.

In the United Kingdom: For a complete list of books available from Penguin in the U.K., please write to *Dept E.P., Penguin Books Ltd, Harmondsworth, Middlesex, UB7 0DA.*

In the United States: For a complete list of books available from Penguin in the U.S., please write to *Consumer Sales, Penguin USA, P.O. Box 999— Dept. 17109, Bergenfield, New Jersey 07621-0120.* VISA and MasterCard holders call 1-800-253-6476 to order all Penguin titles.

In Canada: For a complete list of books available from Penguin in Canada, please write to *Penguin Books Canada Ltd, 10 Alcorn Avenue, Suite 300, Toronto, Ontario, Canada M4V 3B2.*

In Australia: For a complete list of books available from Penguin in Australia, please write to the *Marketing Department, Penguin Books Ltd, P.O. Box 257, Ringwood, Victoria 3134.*

In New Zealand: For a complete list of books available from Penguin in New Zealand, please write to the *Marketing Department, Penguin Books (NZ) Ltd, Private Bag, Takapuna, Auckland 9.*

In India: For a complete list of books available from Penguin, please write to *Penguin Overseas Ltd, 706 Eros Apartments, 56 Nehru Place, New Delhi, 110019.*

In Holland: For a complete list of books available from Penguin in Holland, please write to *Penguin Books Nederland B.V., Postbus 195, NL-1380AD Weesp, Netherlands.*

In Germany: For a complete list of books available from Penguin, please write to *Penguin Books Ltd, Friedrichstrasse 10-12, D-6000 Frankfurt Main 1, Federal Republic of Germany.*

In Spain: For a complete list of books available from Penguin in Spain, please write to *Longman, Penguin España, Calle San Nicolas 15, E-28013 Madrid, Spain.*

In Japan: For a complete list of books available from Penguin in Japan, please write to *Longman Penguin Japan Co Ltd, Yamaguchi Building, 2-12-9 Kanda Jimbocho, Chiyoda-Ku, Tokyo 101, Japan.*